W9-CQC-137

Gourmet Gardening

Gourmet Gardening

Hamilton Tyler

VNR
VAN NOSTRAND REINHOLD COMPANY
NEW YORK CINCINNATI TORONTO LONDON MELBOURNE

Van Nostrand Reinhold Company Regional Offices:
New York Cincinnati Chicago Millbrae Dallas
Van Nostrand Reinhold Company International Offices:
London Toronto Melbourne

Library of Congress Catalog Card Number: 73-149264

Published by Van Nostrand Reinhold Company
450 West 33rd Street, New York, N.Y. 10001

Published simultaneously in Canada by
Van Nostrand Reinhold Ltd.

16 15 14 13 12 11 10 9 8 7 6 5 4 3 2 1

Drawings in Chapter 2 by Charles Hoeppner.
Other drawings by Rosinda Holmes.

Preface

The gourmet is interested in one thing: perfection in taste. And that is why he does well to become a gardener and grow some of his own food. Taste is not particularly important to the commercial growers who supply our supermarkets; they are concerned with yield per acre, and with varieties of fruits and vegetables that ship well or that look good even after months in cold storage. They know that most American shoppers will buy a large bright-red apple with visual appeal rather than a much tastier one half the size. And so even the gourmet with better sense ends up with the showy apple, because that is all that has come to market.

And yet almost all of us have something of the gourmet in us, and eat not just because we are hungry but because we enjoy food. We like variety in our diet, and we are willing to try new foods — the vast number of cookbooks available on foreign cuisines is proof of this. Unfortunately, many of the recipes they offer must be reinterpreted for the American kitchen, which depends so heavily on the American supermarket. One very good book on French cooking suggests using navy beans in recipes where flageolets are called for. The results may be quite satisfactory — but not French.

But the gourmet gardener can grow his own flageolets. He can gather in seeds, bulbs, and tubers from around the world, and if he cooks himself or is married to a skillful cook, he can enjoy authentic dishes made with his international produce, and he can experiment endlessly with original dishes and variations of classics. It is becoming easier all the time to be this sort of gardener. More and more, American firms are making exotic seeds available — and for that matter it is not much more difficult to order seeds from France or England than from an American supplier.

It does take some time and effort to sort out the most desirable varieties. That is why this book has been written. I have grown and eaten almost all the varieties I mention, and I have learned a great deal that I would like to share with other gardeners who enjoy good food. I have by no means written a complete vegetable-garden handbook. I have left out many splendid foods, such as artichokes, simply because their cultivation presents no mysteries. And there are other gaps, since no gardener grows everything and no gourmet likes everything. But I think my experience, as presented in this book, can serve as a guide to other gardeners and help them find a fair course through the labyrinth of unknown or foreign names to a discovery of what is best and most desirable among the edible plants.

I have, of course, devoted several chapters to standard vegetables — carrots, tomatoes, lettuce — and the varieties that make them so much more than standard. Since any gourmet worth his spice is likely to be even more interested in flavoring agents than in basic foodstuffs, I have given nearly as much space to the onion family, herbs, saffron, and curry. Since the gourmet is nothing if not venturesome, I have included a chapter on Oriental foods that can be grown in the garden. A chapter on wine-grape varieties and winemaking is obviously appropriate. There is a chapter on endives and mushrooms, which can keep the gourmet gardener active after the harvest season, and a chapter on saving and storing your own seeds in preparation for your next planting season. Finally, I have listed some books that will help the serious gardener learn more, and some sources of seeds and equipment that will enable the beginner to get started.

Good appetite!

Contents

Seed packets from here and abroad. (Joyce R. Wilson photo)

1 Basics: Seeds, Soils, and Attention to Detail

Anyone who is already a vegetable gardener should not suddenly decide one spring to plant only gourmet varieties. Start slow, but be sure; try a few varieties first. The new is always chancy as well as exciting. Sometimes things will grow better than you expected, but more often testing and trying are necessary. Most exotic varieties are as easy to grow as the familiar old ones, once you know the proper planting dates and cultivation methods, but such knowledge can't be acquired overnight.

On the other hand, don't stick to one variety of seed simply because a neighbor states it is the only one available or the only one that will thrive in the locality. Many people will swear that there are only two kinds of green beans: 'Kentucky Wonders' and 'Blue Lakes.' But some gourmet gardeners could take you into their gardens and ask you to taste perhaps twenty varieties of green beans. As you bit into first one and then another green bean, discovering a nutty flavor here, a sweetness there, you would be surprised and delighted to discover how different plain old green beans can be. The whole purpose of gourmet gardening is to learn to recognize and use the subtle distinctions between varieties of the same vegetable.

SPECIAL SEEDS

Most American seed growers aim at a mass market that will buy their packets from the seed racks in grocery, hardware, and other stores. Naturally they don't want to send out a little-known item and then have to discard it unsold at the end of the season. Fortunately, many seedsmen are now putting out at least a few unusual varieties, and these seeds often can be found in nurseries and feed stores.

The mail-order seed firms are even more likely to list a few special varieties along with the standard ones. I was surprised to get a Breck's of Boston catalog and find both 'Carrot Sucram' and 'Beet Spinel' listed. There are also smaller seedsmen, like Nichols Garden Nursery or Harry E. Saier, who make a point of importing many European and Oriental varieties of seed. These are all new and welcome trends.

One reason we do not have a diversity of seed varieties in the United States is that the small market garden is almost a thing of the past. Time was when an immigrant or second-generation native of Italian, French, Dutch, German, or Japanese extraction could maintain three or four acres of many kinds of plants, including those varieties he remembered from his home country. He could send back to relatives, friends, and firms he was accustomed to dealing with for the special seeds.

Now, in place of the small market garden, we grow most of our vegetables in immense plantings that resemble the collective farms of Russia. One vast patch may run into thousands of acres, all planted to the same crop. These huge farms are frequently owned by a conglomerate that has ventured into agriculture as one of its sidelines, and

this kind of operation hardly encourages diversity in vegetable produce.

Everyone today, from the researcher to the seedsman to the grower, is trying to get earlier crops, more production per acre, and standard varieties. Perhaps the consumer is the only one who can reverse the trend, as he becomes aware of the hazards of the pesticides used in commercial agriculture and begins to demand an organically grown product — and is willing to pay a premium price for one.

The small market garden still thrives in many places in Europe. The shopper can choose freshly picked varieties either in the garden or from a farmer's stand in the market. European hybridizers and seedsmen are keenly aware of the demand for specialized varieties and have worked toward that end, and that is why so many of the varieties mentioned in this book are European.

Ordering a carton of seeds from Europe is not really much more difficult than domestic mail ordering. It requires the foresight to send for a catalog in early winter so that you have time to choose what you want and receive it before planting time. It is wise to order early, since shipment may be slow.

The prices of many seeds are modest, and the quantity you get is most generous, which will probably compensate for the postage. Once you buy seeds from firms like Sutton's and Thompson & Morgan in England and Vilmorin and Delbard in France, their beautifully illustrated catalogs will arrive automatically in winter, in time to let you choose both flower and vegetable seeds. If you forget to order early, use airmail both ways.

(Opposite) Seeds may be the end product as well as the beginning. At the back of the home-food altar are jars of beans and dried mushrooms. In the center foreground are items for home-ground curry: coriander and cardamon seed, red-hot peppers, and garlic, with the wooden mortars in which they will be ground. At left is oregano, and to the right is Chinese parsley. (Joyce R. Wilson photo)

There is a slight problem about how much money to send. The English catalogs include a chart that allows you to calculate the price in dollars. To convert francs to dollars, consult a local bank. You don't have to be exact since these firms will bill you for any reasonable amount that is due, or credit your account for any overpayment.

SOILS

Most trees will get along in just about any soil, and many shrubs and most annual and perennial flowers will make do with indifferent footing. They do have individual preferences, but they will survive and even bloom a bit in a variety of soil conditions. Vegetables are more particular.

Anything to be eaten should be grown quickly and lushly. Some of the seasoning plants are exceptions, but for most vegetables rapid, unchecked growth is desirable. A stunted plant will do nothing for your table, even if you finally get it to produce. The main causes of retarded growth are unfavorable weather and poor soil. All you can do about weather is to judge the proper time to plant and supply extra moisture if a dry period lasts too long. But soil is entirely within your control, if you are willing to make the extra effort.

Probably every gardener has read on the back of a seed packet some instruction like "Sow in a rich, friable soil." There may be a few places where the planting ground is already rich and friable, but in most areas this quality must be built up, often painfully. When working as a professional gardener, I was always surprised that people would buy plant after plant for the same difficult spot without thinking of enriching the soil, except by commercial fertilizers.

"Rich" means, primarily, that the soil is high in organic content. Commercial fertilizers are worthless, unless the soil has a high organic content, because it is the soil microorganisms that transform chemical matter into foods that plants can use. "Friable" means that the soil is loose and can be worked easily. Friability, which like richness results from organic matter, allows seeds to germinate and roots to grow easily. If root crops such as carrots have to bore their way down through unfriable soil, their fiber content is increased as they strain. The more fiber there is, the less succulence and sugar.

Composts. An iris may bloom on a clay hillside, but you will get no tender vegetables there. To grow vegetables in any but the best soil, some kind of compost is necessary. Manures, particularly the gleanings from stables and barns, are ideal if they are first allowed to decompose. They contain a high percentage of straw, hay, and perhaps the sawdust that was used as bedding, which increases the friability of the soil. Beside loosening soil structure, manure composts feed the fungi and bacteria at work in the garden earth.

The gardener with a small amount of land can also buy packaged composts, manure, and black peat. Manure from small stock, such as sheep or rabbits, lacks the bulky material that loosens soil. Its nutrient content is higher than stable manure but is not in a form that plants can use immediately. Chicken manure is rich in nitrogen but should never be applied to the vegetable garden directly; it should be composted with garden trimmings. In such a mixture, the high nitrogen content will help transform the scraps and garbage into soil builders.

A compost heap is virtually a necessity. You can make it from autumn leaves and lawn clippings, or the trimmings from vegetables. These wastes can be combined with manures (or any nitrogen substitute, such as cottonseed meal), a layer of dirt every 6 or 8 inches, and weeds as you have them. The result, when ripe, will be a perfect medium for growing plants.

If you are growing vegetables on a city porch or in other limited space, a real compost pile is not in order. There are substitutes, such as peat moss and perlite, that work to break up the soil in small pots or container plantings. Both are lightweight, an advantage that will appeal to anyone who has made a rooftop or porch garden or has tried to shift an earth-filled tub from one place to another. However, neither peat moss nor perlite contains plant nutrients, and peat moss is highly acid, which must be corrected by adding lime. Since these additions to a soil mix add no nutrient value, bone meal, blood meal, and cottonseed meal have to be added before planting.

However, another compost substitute, sterilized steer manure, adds food as well as friability and is also light in weight. Few, if any, weeds will result from adding it to the soil, since it is sterile.

GROWING WITH A RUSH

Many vegetables, such as peppers, suffer from any check in their growth. If a check meant only that the crop would be later or less bountiful, it would be a small matter, but that is not the way vegetables grow. Impoverished seedlings will not produce vegetables of the same quality as those that are grown straight through with a rush, and often it is best to add them to the compost heap.

To some extent the factors that determine plant growth can be controlled to prevent checks. For example, to start early seedlings, bottom heat may be essential. Dual electric wires (available from Park Seed Co., and others) that can be plugged into any circuit are inexpensive and easy to use. They are buried in sand under the seed flats and maintain a constant temperature below. Once the seedlings are up, an overhead light bulb maintains a relatively

Bean poles waiting for spring, while in the background greens and alliums hold the field. Beans, tomatoes, and other common summer vegetables cannot be planted until all danger of frost is past.

constant heat, which encourages the seedlings. If these arrangements sound like too much effort, it is best to wait until later in the season to germinate your seeds. Unfortunately, some of the best vegetables are the first, and if you wait you will miss them.

BLANCHING

Even as plants are growing they may be improved in tenderness. Some vegetables, such as celery and leeks, need blanching or "earthing up." The earth is gradually drawn up around the plants. With celery, the earth can be carried clear up to the leaves by the time it is ready for harvest. It is not for the whiteness that one blanches, but for the tenderness that results when the edible parts are kept in darkness. This is why the inner shoots of celery bought in the market are so much tenderer than the outer ones.

Most chicories are improved by blanching. On heading types you can simply twist a wire tie around the head to keep the leaves tightly together. If they are earthed up it is wise to use some sort of collar to keep the soil from getting into the heart. Once the plant is well started it is possible to blanch it by placing a flowerpot over it for part of the day. Chicories seem to be more flavorful and less bitter when grown with minimum sunlight. Second-year roots of any variety will leaf out in total darkness.

PICKING AT THE PEAK

Excellence in home-garden vegetables is obtained by paying attention to all the details — seed varieties, soils, planting times, watering, ensuring rapid growth, and so on. But this excellence is wasted unless you know when to harvest. The best of varieties will soon become no better than commonplace if they are allowed to pass their point of perfection. So you must learn to tell when each has reached its delicate peak.

Dry beans and herb seeds are at their best when fully mature, although *flageolets* are also delicious when shelled green. The same is not true of the famous French dry bean 'Comtesse de Chambord': it is only perfect at full maturity.

Some vegetables give visible signs, such as the size of fruit or seeds, to show that they are ready for harvesting. Most summer squashes can be judged this way. For perfection, the small zucchinis the French call *courgettes* must be picked when no bigger than the thumb, since they should be fried whole like little pig sausages. If they are allowed to grow bigger, the result is mediocre taste and texture. There are both old and new hybrid F_1 summer squashes that are far superior when medium-sized. When summer squashes grow slightly larger, they are good stuffed (see recipes in Chapter 3), but when they get very large they are only suitable for the compost heap. Winter squashes are not difficult to judge — they are good to full maturity. But you will have to decide when they are ripe enough and, if they need more time, whether there is danger of bottom rot or a heavy freeze.

Root crops give hardly any signs of perfect ripeness. A carrot or beet will look much the same on the outside whether it has been in the ground the two months or so needed to ripen it, or whether it has been there three times as long. In that case, it will be no better than those in markets, even if you started with a superior strain.

For those and similar plants you need to keep a garden notebook or at least a dated label on each row, especially in the warmer sections of the West and South, where planting of some kinds can be done throughout the year. Relying on memory is no good, particularly when the plantings are being rotated — no one wants a whole bed of carrots at the same time. A record of dates gives the gardener a clue to the peak of excellence, and if he keeps it for several years he will learn much about the best planting dates in the unique climate of his own garden.

Plant growth time is quite variable. Most of the information printed on seed packets and in catalogs about the number of days to maturity is based on a planting at the peak of spring, under optimum weather conditions. At that season everything takes off with a burst of vigor, but summer plantings of the same seeds are likely to take many more days of growing time to mature, and in fall and winter the growth rate will be even slower. When winter-forcing vegetables under glass for your own use, all the variables become more difficult to judge; it will take more than one season of gardening experience to learn when you will get the best crop.

All the extra thought is worth it, if you are aiming for the best. Try a lettuce at its peak and later one of the same variety and same row that is about to bolt. You will have no doubt that there is a shadow of mediocrity that stands just behind the mark of excellence.

2 Container Gardening

Most of my vegetables are grown in the open ground, but I've found that there are quite a few that do better in some kind of container, even when ample space is available. By using containers, gardeners limited to small areas such as porches, patios, sun rooms, or odd corners of the lawn can enjoy a garden for gourmets. Some people are not willing to sacrifice space in their flower gardens for the sake of a few edibles and yet want tasty vegetables, and containers are an excellent way out of this dilemma, too. Containers provide extra gardening space set on window sills, hung on fences or walls, or set out in the sun on porches and patios. Even though they contain edible food rather than what we think of as ornamental plants, the containers come in so many shapes, sizes, and materials that you will be able to find one to fit in almost anywhere.

Intensively cultivated, these small gardening areas will produce enough choice food for home needs. Bulk is never the goal of the gourmet gardener — no one wants to eat 10 pounds of even the choicest green beans every day for half the year.

WHAT TO GROW

Although you can hardly do much with corn plants in a small garden, there are some very fine squashes that will adapt perfectly. The species *Lageneria longissima* will ramble along a fence for 20 feet or more and blossom out in a succession of ephemeral white blooms that resemble Japanese irises. They are nearly as beautiful, and at night they have the mothlike character of moon flowers.

When picked young, the fruit is a summer squash of utmost delicacy. It can be grown in a very narrow space against a fence, where it will produce blooms and fruit throughout the summer. The musky flavor may not please everyone at first taste, but that is its only disadvantage.

A few pots of chives or a tub of parsley will look attractive no matter where you put them. They will do well along a narrow path or walk leading to the kitchen, even if the neighboring house or apartment is too near to provide anything but a minimum of sunlight. They are even more useful on the steps to the kitchen door or in a window box, where the cook can reach out and gather the herbs.

Kitchen window boxes can be attractively edged with a trailing herb like thyme, or perhaps ivy geraniums to cheer things up. Petunias can trail over the edge without crowding the culinary items behind.

Less-common plants like shallots grow equally well in a window box or tub. The smaller multiplying onions do even better in a window box than shallots, and you can cut the tops as needed, or even divide and replant a few at a time. Sorrel is ideal for either window boxes or tubs since three plants will supply most needs.

Any kind of a tub from 12 to 16 inches in

Containers are ideal for many herbs, such as this true tarragon plant. This 18-inch barrel half will supply family needs for most of the year and provide root divisions for friends. (Matt Barr photo)

diameter will do for specialty crops, such as multiplying onions, shallots, and many herbs. Even salad greens will grow in these small containers. A combination planting — for example, one plant each of sweet marjoram, chives, and sorrel — will do very well together in a 12- or 14-inch tub.

Rosemary and the true bay laurel become large-sized shrubs in time, and so they should be potted in bigger and bigger containers as they grow. Half of a 25-gallon barrel that has been cut in two will keep both plants happy for many years. There are also a number of perennial herbs, like tarragon and oregano, that can be grown in 6-inch flower pots. Although flower pots are ideal for the smaller herbs, 12- and 14-inch clay pots are needed for most vegetables. The pots are heavy and subject to breakage, but you can grow a wonderful column of winter tomatoes in one if there is a sun room or greenhouse available.

Being annuals, most of the superior vegetables are not suitable for tub or pot culture. For winter greenhouse work they can be grown with a high stake, but in the regular season there is no reason not to spread out a little, while still using containers. A narrow box built at the base of a fence makes a very good container for peas, beans, or tomatoes.

SPECIAL SOILS AND UNUSUAL WEATHER CONDITIONS

Kitchen convenience is not the only advantage of container gardening. Because there is so little of it, the soil in containers can be selected and perfected. A farmer starts with his basic soil type, whatever it is, and then selects crops that will do well in it. He can improve the soil, but it is a difficult and costly process; the number of tons of sand necessary to change a heavy soil into a light one is almost beyond imagination. (Where I grew up, the soil was nothing but sand, which grew some crops superbly and others not at all.)

The gourmet gardener is not interested in this kind of monoculture. What he needs is a variety of every kind of soil for a garden that is to be all-inclusive. Some plants like to grow in slightly acid soil — parsley, tomato, turnips; others won't tolerate it — beets, carrots, leeks, chard. Fertilizer requirements also differ. Peas, beans, and other legumes require less nitrogen than the rest of the green plants since they can manufacture their own; root crops need more than the usual amount of potash, which stimulates root growth. In any kind of container the soil can be tailored to fit the plant, and it is no great problem to renew or replace the growing medium entirely from time to time.

Equally important, container growing allows the gardener to adapt to unusual weather conditions. A farmer takes what weather he gets — and for the most part, he doesn't like it. The container gardener can always substitute a counter-climate by moving pots and smaller tubs with the seasons, to take advantage of sun and shade as they are needed. Rain is a great blessing unless it comes in torrents, and then it is handy to be able to move containers under some protection. During unseasonable frosts, pots and tubs can be set on an indoor porch for a night or two.

Even fixed containers are useful for weather control. The cold frame, a bed that has a wooden border with glass over the top, and the hotbed, a box with glass over the top and bottom heat, are commonly used protections against cold weather. Beds that have wooden borders may be used all year by covering them with either glass or cloth, as the season or temperature demands. Put a few 2 x 4s across the bed, resting on its edges, and lay the

(Opposite) Container boxes in use and in construction. These 10-foot beds allow one to mix a perfect soil for almost any plant. (Joyce R. Wilson photo)

glass — any old window sash will do — over the boards when needed. This is no hotbed, but it may give plants several weeks of extra growing time on each end of the season. A cloth or reed cover over one of these container beds will provide protection from pelting rains and shade from the sun. Cloth can be bought with weaves designed to filter out 30, 50, or 70 percent of the sunlight.

Very small architectural areas usually have the advantage of being surrounded by neighboring buildings, garages, or fences. The old interior Spanish patio or the Roman atrium must have been ideal for growing choice plants in containers, but any confined space will serve as well to blunt the wind and retain more heat than open ground. Take advantage of south walls, overhanging eaves, and outbuildings. Mobile plants can be shuffled in and out of any old shed or garage when weather threatens. The old-fashioned sun porch was not only a splendid piece of architectural genius, but a boon to container gardeners; my grandmother kept hers stocked with coleus, caladiums, and geraniums. The sun porch would have served equally well for kitchen plants and herbs.

SHAPES FOR CONTAINERS

Boxes. Plant boxes come in all shapes, and it doesn't seem to matter much what the dimensions are, they all work well. I prefer containers small enough to be shifted about easily, or fixed boxes that become part of the landscape. There is nothing quite so handsome as a clay or glazed pot, but they are heavier and more easily broken than wooden ones. Wood containers are light and easily handled; they won't break if tipped over, and therefore it is safe to turn them upside down to knock out the soil when replanting.

Landscape architects often arrange long boxes in tiers of two or three, so that low-growing crops planted on the lower level will dress up the leggy stems of stalk or vine varieties planted above. Chard or lettuce and peas or beans would make good foils for one another. In such boxes an ornamental like nasturtium or alyssum can be planted along the edge. Even a climbing ornamental can be used to camouflage the bare stems of vegetables if judicious pruning is done. The effect of orange nasturtiums grown with one of the purple-podded beans such as 'Blue Coco' or 'Blue Queen' is strikingly colorful.

On flat ground or against a fence, two levels of narrow boxes, not more than 10 inches wide, seem to work the best. On sloping ground, terracing with a series of larger containers not only keeps the topsoil in place, but the containers can be arranged so that you don't have to get down on your hands and knees to weed or cultivate. If the lower side is made out of old railroad ties, perhaps four high, the resulting bed will be easy to work.

Some illustrations are given here for boxes that can be built at home. Nail the sides together securely and use galvanized nails in construction — brass screws are even better if you are that diligent. Always drill holes — about ¾-inch will do — in the bottom of any wooden container for drainage. For shallots, chives, green onion sets, lettuce, and some of the other greens, these boxes can be as shallow as 8 inches. Because chicories have long tap roots, they are not good for these boxes, but there are varieties of carrots that are round and will grow in shallow soil.

Shallow boxes that are 24 inches square are still light enough to be shifted about easily by the gardener, and will turn out a surprising amount of good things to eat. These boxes can be combined with longer and deeper ones to provide attractive configurations in a small space.

L-Shaped Containers. A variation of the plant box,

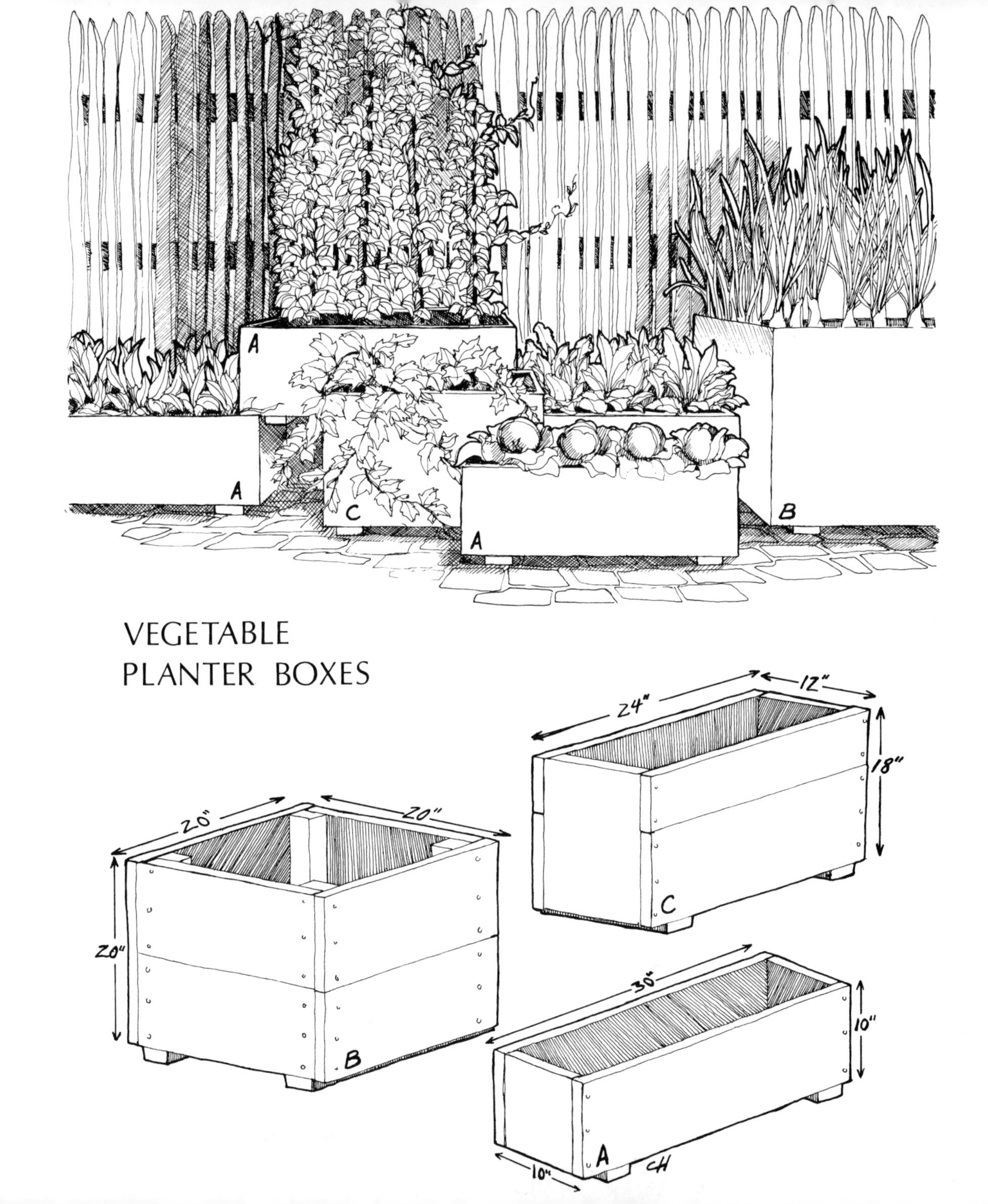

VEGETABLE PLANTER BOXES

TERRACED CONTAINERS

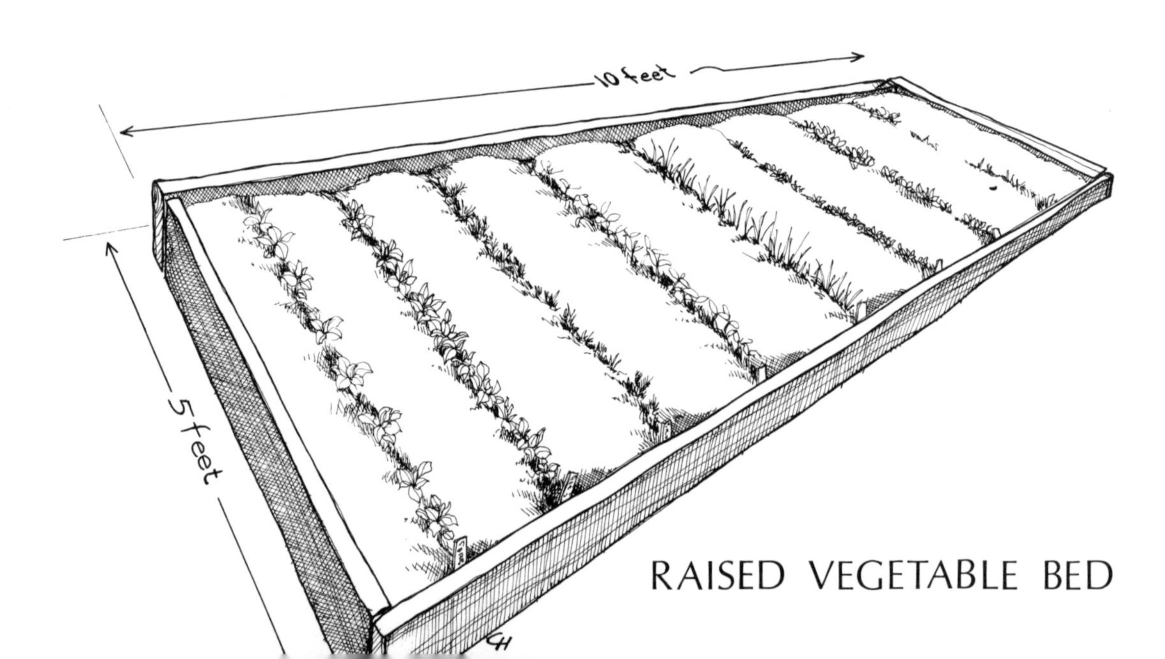

RAISED VEGETABLE BED

'L' SHAPED CONTAINER

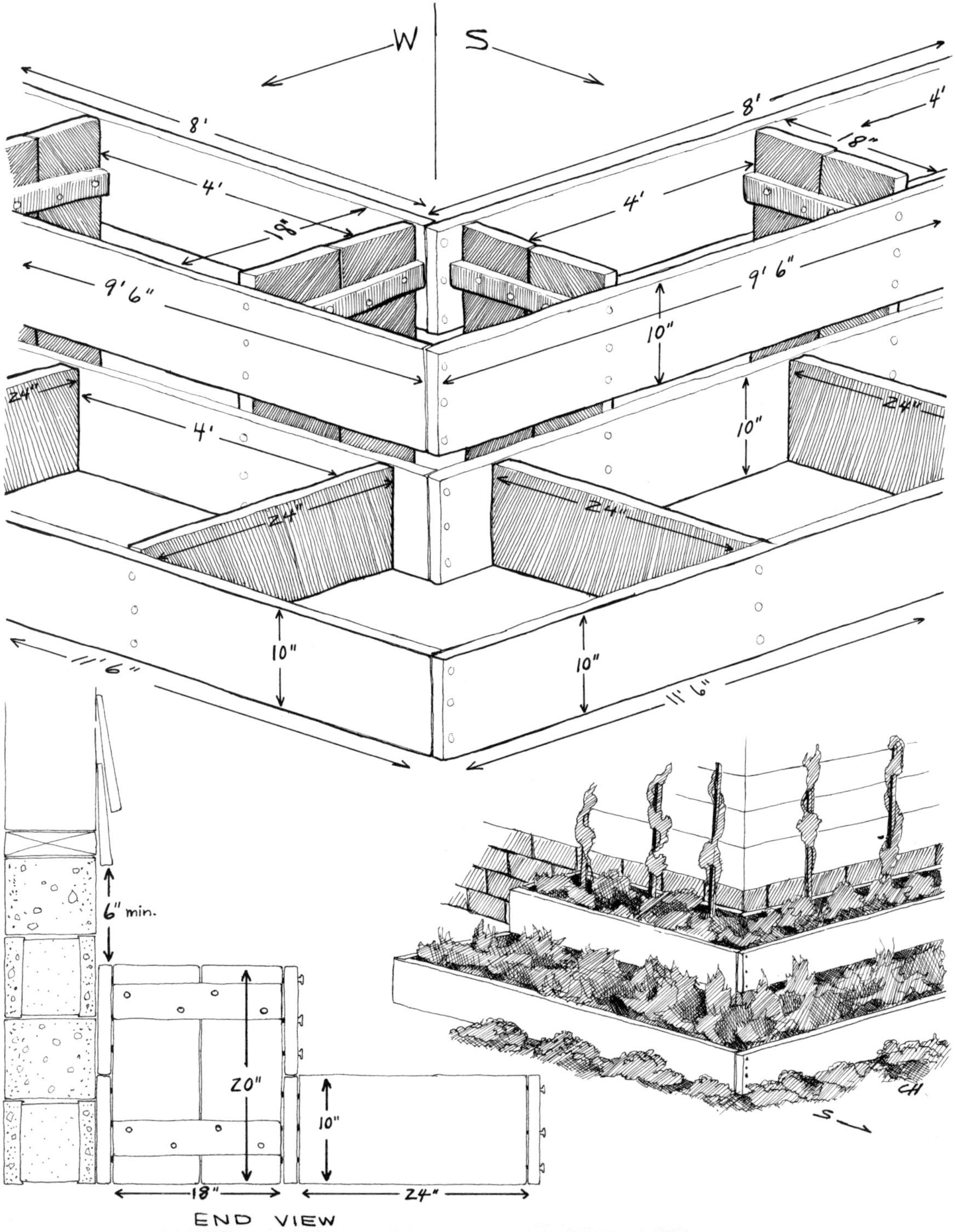

W
S
8'
8'
4'
4'
18"
4'
18"
9' 6"
9' 6"
10"
24"
10"
4'
24"
24"
24"
10"
10"
11' 6"
11' 6"
6" min.
20"
10"
18"
24"
END VIEW
S
CH

an L-shaped container made of wood and concrete, stone, or bricks provides a gardening area against the corner of a house or garage. These beds can be designed to fit the inside of an L-shaped area of a house or to wrap around a corner. The advantage of L-shaped containers is that they provide varied growing conditions. Some vegetables like full heat, while others prefer shade or only morning sun. Okra, for example, will thrive against the south wall of a house, where heat is multiplied as it reflects from the building on a summer afternoon, and chervil, in the same container, will do well around the corner with a cool and shady east exposure.

Because of the termite problem, the back walls of the container should be made of concrete, concrete blocks, or brick, and all wood should be kept at least 6 inches above the soil level. The outer walls of the container can be made of wood if the container is angled around a garden shed, but around the corner of a house brick is much more attractive. An upper level 18 inches wide and a lower level 24 inches wide make an aesthetically pleasing container, still narrow enough so that you can reach to the back of the bed.

There are many ways to vary the pattern by constructing divided and multiple-level containers. When you do the work yourself you can change the proportions if they don't look right. Complex arrangements make a maximum use of minimum space, but a quasi-cubist design that has gone wrong can ruin the natural perspectives of any garden, large or small. If you want to try multiple levels and divisions, build with rock and no mortar. Even an amateur mason can shift a dry rock wall around until the structural relationships look right.

Tubs and Barrel Halves. Many people who enjoy good food are are in no position to undertake elaborate construction projects around their homes. Younger gourmets are likely to be renters, or, if not, may be planning to move before long. In either case the temporary rather than the permanent container is called for; tubs can always be moved when you do.

Tubs are perhaps simpler than barrel halves since they were designed for the gardener. Tubs are made of redwood or cypress, usually with eight sides that taper down like a flower pot. A common size is 12 to 14 inches at the mouth, which is big enough to hold anything from a pole of beans to a bed of parsley. Garden-supply houses also supply a metal frame with three castors so that the pot can be rolled or pushed around without lifting.

Barrels and kegs come in many sizes, shapes, and materials. Used ones are often inexpensive. Wine barrels are usually made from oak. Nail kegs are made from soft wood and will not last longer than ten years when filled with soil. When filled with water — you may want to grow cress and ornamentals in such a water garden — a barrel half will last almost indefinitely. However, it is a good idea to coat the inside of a barrel to be filled with soil with a fungicide like copper-green.

A 50-gallon barrel cut in half will be about 24 inches in diameter, and is suitable for anything up to a full-size laurel tree or the junipers that produce edible berries. One window sash laid over the top will turn the barrel half into an early-season bed for many vegetable varieties.

Unfortunately, even half of a 50-gallon barrel is a heavy object. A lighter, 25-gallon barrel half measures about 15 inches across the mouth, and holds more soil than the standard nursery tub. Smaller barrels and kegs permit more decorative arrangements while still supplying an excellent environment and hand-tailored soil for a few choice vegetables.

Other Containers. Lightweight Styrofoam pots have recently appeared on the market. Unfortunately, the big ones tend to blow over if the plant grows high

VEGETABLE CONTAINERS

enough to become top-heavy. Dogs will munch on the rims, and the rims will break if you aren't careful when lifting the pot, since the material has little strength.

Some people use the strawberry jar for vegetables, but it should be saved for decorative plants or for growing strawberries. You can achieve the same effect by using mounds that are made with concentric rims, the whole forming a little terraced knoll. These mounds will grow more strawberries or vegetables than ordinary containers, but there is often a design problem in fitting a 6-foot circle into a small square or rectangular area. The result may look like a temporary booth in a flower show.

Handmade pottery containers are better-looking than ordinary clay pots and serve the purpose. You can make an attractive kitchen display of these pots and still grow useful seasonings, like chives and herbs, on your window sills. If you have many pots, all will not fit on the sill at the same time. By rotating them weekly, each will have the benefit of fresh air and direct light, and none will have to stay indoors, near the cooking gas, too long.

Despite all these advantages of gardening in containers, it is still desirable to have half an acre of open ground to give you room for experimentation. Some ordinary vegetables, like corn, require more space than the largest container can provide. And, because gourmet varieties may not suit all tastes, the curious gardener needs enough room to make a mistake once in a while.

3 Lowly Vegetables in Gourmet Varieties: Root Crops and Squashes

It would be very hard to think of anything more ordinary to grow in your vegetable garden than carrots, beets, turnips, and summer squash. Nevertheless, the difference between varieties is extraordinary — perhaps more so than in any of the other vegetables mentioned in this book, if taste is the main concern. Most people take the basic roots and squashes for granted, thinking of each kind as a basic fact. In this country carrots are simply bought as carrots; I have never seen a sign telling the buyer what kinds they were. But in Europe the distinctions are important. The home gardener here, unlike the consumer, has a complete range of choices available and should take advantage of it.

CARROTS

With the exception of potatoes, carrots are probably the commonest of all vegetables in the United States. There is never a market that doesn't have them all year, just like potatoes. This is a fairly recent development. In fact, before the seventeenth century carrots were regarded as a wild herb with medicinal values. Then some Dutch breeder thought of improving the roots for their food value. Holland is still the source of many of the best new carrot varieties.

The triumph of the carrot on the marketplace is partly attributable to the fact that commercial kinds have a long "shelf life." Carrots are always available because they handle well, and last. In a market you will likely find 'Chantenay,' 'Danvers,' and more lately, 'Imperator. One reason these varieties keep well is that they have a high fiber content — which the home gardener doesn't want. Another reason for their success is that they grow uniformly large even though some are slim and others plump. From the farmer's standpoint, this means many more tons from his field, and who could blame him for growing them? However, for at least half the year a home gardener doesn't need the keeping advantage of a fibrous root because he digs carrots just before eating them. He doesn't need size either, as that generally detracts from quality (there are exceptions among some of the larger varieties if they are grown quickly).

Within any variety of carrots the young ones taste the best, even among choice specialties, because the sugar that makes a carrot sweet begins to be replaced by fiber as it ages. Fiber is also increased when carrots are grown in a stiff soil; the root has to toughen itself in order to make its way downward. Below I will describe a special carrot bed in which the soil is adapted to growing only the tenderest and preventing fiber buildup.

Some years ago I shared the opinion of a garden writer of 1866 who stated, "Though not relished by all palates, carrots are extensively employed for culinary purposes. . . . They are also considered valuable for almost all descriptions of livestock." He further pointed out that carrots were not only nutritious as feed for dairy cows but that they

The special enclosed bed allowed me to grow these carrots in ideal soil. (J. Williamson photo)

imparted their yellow color to the butter.

I recall feeding a 20-ton truckload of carrots to a dairy herd, and they did indeed enjoy every mouthful. In fact, the cows looked and sounded so happy that I tried one! This only confirmed my impression that the goodness of carrots depended mostly on how much butter could be worked into the dish — in part a dairyman's prejudice — and the topping of mint or some other fine herb.

But because my wife likes them, self-defense led me to some carrot research. People back from a trip to Europe always mentioned the marvelous little carrots, round like ours but finger-size. Since then I have grown more than twenty kinds, mostly European. It didn't take long to discover that some of the special varieties of this most ordinary vegetable could be an epicure's delight and that butter had very little to do with the taste.

A Special Carrot Bed. Besides choosing a good carrot variety, your soil and water conditions must be exactly right for perfection and tenderness. Any light soil will grow carrots, but a special plot or box that has been redone for the project will produce the finest. Get three 2″ x 6″ boards (redwood, cedar, or cypress), 8 or 10 feet long. Cut one board in half to form the ends, and nail all the boards together with large galvanized nails. Stakes at the corners add extra strength.

Within this rectangular box work up a soil mix of one-third soil, one-third sand, and one-third compost. As these ingredients are being mixed, sprinkle in a 5-pound sack of bonemeal. The soil is the easiest to work with, for the borders can be sunken an inch or two or placed on a slight incline where there will be plenty of earth. Sand is the rub in terms of labor; if the contents of the bed are dug to a foot in depth, which they should be, a 5′ x 10′ box will hold 50 cubic feet of material, a third of it sand. This means a bit of drudgery with a wheelbarrow, but the project doesn't have to be done in a day, and the results will last indefinitely.

If you don't have compost, a substitute can be made by mixing leafmold and peat moss, or well-rotted sawdust. Never use manure because it causes forking of the roots. Use wood ashes if available since they add potash to the soil, thus promoting root growth. Greensand and granite dust are other good sources of potash. After the first year you will need to add one of these ingredients, bonemeal being the easiest, to replenish the soil. In a loose and sandy bed such as this one, nutrients leach away more rapidly than in open ground.

A small carrot bed will produce more choice carrots year-round than any family can eat. For early- and late-season crops, add a window sash over the box on cold nights. If the rows are planted in the short dimension of the rectangle, there will be nine, which means that a succession of harvesting is possible. There won't be many carrots in any one row, but there will always be enough, and of different varieties. Carrots will keep very well in this sandy bed, but it is not intended as a root cellar; all you want is a few of the choicest at their prime.

Starting is something of a problem because if all nine rows are planted to carrots they will mature at about the same time. A few rows should be planted to green onions, radishes, and so forth until a succession is under way. Most carrots take two and a half months to mature (or a little less in spring), so planting at two- or three-week intervals works out about right. As you pull the radishes, another row of carrots is added, continuing to the green onions and lettuce. At that point you will be pulling the tenderest of carrots and replanting.

Varieties: The Nantes Group. Probably the standard for this group is the French one called *touchon.* It is excellent, and seed is available in this country (Nichols). These larger "stump-rooted" carrots have smaller brothers and sisters. 'Early Nantes' has long been popular in England, and there is an improved form of better flavor called 'Tip Top.' Oddly enough, it is only listed in French catalogs, so presumably the British like the older ones.

The Dutch have developed a very superior form called *sucram*, which is another dwarf Nantes. *Sucram* means sweet; Van der Ploeg gets the credit for developing the variety. When pulled at about the size of a wife's little finger, it is incredibly good. When left to grow larger, like the stump-rooted fingers of the master, it is no better than *touchon.* These litle carrots should always be cooked whole and the skin then slipped off.

Forcing Carrots. Carrots are rather hardy, although, unlike salsify, they will not do much in frozen ground. But given a little encouragement, they can be started under glass as early as February, or if fall-planted and protected they will mature in midwinter. Quite a few varieties have been developed for that purpose by European market gardeners. One of the best is the finger-shaped 'Amstel,' a Dutch introduction. 'French Horn' and 'Amsterdam Forcing' are also very quick-growing, tiny carrots with any number of secondary varieties.

There are also little carrots that come in odd shapes. 'Paris Forcing' is like a spool of thread; 'Dutch Scarlet Horn' looks like a bit of a thumb. Keep in mind that these small carrots need not be grown under glass, even though they do suit that purpose; outside they do perfectly well.

There is one other carrot worth mentioning since the name crops up on importers' lists: 'Carotte de Meaux.' In some lists it will be described as having purple foliage. The lower stems and shoulders are of a purplish hue, but it is not a carrot for the selective gardener. It is a very good winter keeper and quite all right in flavor but not up to the choice ones.

BEETS

There are many kinds of carrots, but only a few varieties of beets are worth considering. Among these are old standards like 'Detroit,' which has progeny all over the world. There are several others that are good and well known, but we are after the little-known and the best. Van der Ploeg in Holland developed the baby beet called 'Beet Spinel' (Brecks or Nichols). It should be eaten when scarcely larger than a walnut and can be cooked with its red-ribbed dark-green leaves.

Of the larger beets the carrot-shaped 'Crapaudine' is superb. It is nearly standard in France, and seed is available from Nichols, without sending abroad. The skin is a very blackish red. A third extraordinary beet is 'Longue Vertes' (Nichols). The root is not as tasty as the 'Crapaudine,' but its leafage is abundant and unequaled as a cooked green. The root is long and shaped like a submarine, and it tends to grow on top of the ground if the soil is loose. It is ideal for pickling since it can be sliced like a sausage. (For whatever it is worth, our domestic rabbit thinks that it is the best thing in the garden next to a young carrot!)

TURNIPS

Like beets, turnips enjoy a richer soil than that described for the carrot bed, particularly if you plan to use the tops as greens. Consequently I mix in both bonemeal and cottonseed meal when making up the bed. Turnips and beets do very well in the same bed, since turnips are strictly a cool-weather crop while beets will stand some summer heat.

There are very few specialty turnips. The best is from Sakata in Japan, called 'Tokyo Cross' because it is an F_1 hybrid. The little globes are perfectly white and round. They should be eaten when no larger than a golf ball, which is easy to tell since they grow almost entirely above ground, sending only the little tail down below. They are so good that they are rapidly becoming a staple in this country; most seedsmen stock them.

The yellow turnips have been around for at least a century. Unlike the yellow beets, which are grown only for cattle, they are perfection. In a canvass of English gardeners, the variety called 'Golden Ball' got a three-star rating for flavor; this means that the agreement was almost unanimous. The Burpee Seed Company has a version under the same name in this country — in England it is often disguised under the name of 'Orange Jelly' and in France as 'Jaune Boule d'or.' So far as I can tell they are the same, although each seedsman selects his own strain.

There are some black-skinned and long-rooted turnips such as *caluire* and *noir longue*, but I have never discovered any particular flavor virtue in these. 'Shogoin' is the oriental variety grown exclusively for its greens, and it is without equal for that purpose. A garden-grown and early-harvested turnip of a standard variety such as white or red 'Milan' is extremely fine.

Many people object to turnips, but that is because they simply boil up the roots. For a change try slicing them and sprinkling a bit of home-grown and roasted curry powder over the top as they are being fried in olive oil; there will never be any of these left on the platter.

SQUASH

Squash enjoys the full light and heat of summer, unlike the "underground" crops. Some root crops tolerate the onslaught of the dog days, but they don't really prefer it. Given enough water and a rich soil, squash can endure even a burning climate. A temperature of 110°F. only makes their fruits ripen faster if they have all the water they can possibly use.

Everyone is familiar with the general types of summer squash, but there are some that are very little known here. *Lagenaria longissima* was mentioned earlier for its climbing habit and beautiful blooms. It is a relative of the African bottle-gourd

This long, thin squash, *Lagenaria longissima,* is a relative of the bottle gourd and has a rather musky taste. (Matt Barr photo)

(Opposite) Avacodella squash, sometimes called Argentine marrow, is as round as a pumpkin. (Matt Barr photo)

types, but this squash is good as food. The flavor is slightly musky, which is in its favor, as no mushrooms have to be added to the dish. There is a challenge in these unknowns from a cook's standpoint: *Lagenaria* has a firm texture and a different taste, so you have to think about what herbs and other vegetables should be combined to bring out its best.

Another little-known squash is the Argentine marrow, or *avacodella.* The latter name stems from the fact that when cooked and cut into wedges, *avacodella* looks almost exactly like an avocado as prepared for a salad. The vines are very large, so space will be needed. Its fruit is produced in clusters; they should be harvested when they are 6-inch spheres. To prepare the fruit, quarter and parboil them in the skin for only a few minutes — test and taste. When the center is done, the outside hide peels off readily, leaving a two-toned green core. These slices, however you cut them, need nothing more for taste, but a few threads of red pimiento laid across them will make a very fine color pattern. A French summer squash is called *coureuse* (the word means "runner"). It looks like zucchini in shape, but it is either white or the palest green in color. Its flavor is totally bland, which suggests that it would make a fine vehicle if hooked up to something, but what horse that is I haven't yet discovered. Tomato and basil help a great deal, but as I like the rather wild green flavor of the following group, there seems little reason to take *coureuse* out of the experimental garden.

Zucchini. "Zucchini" is the Italian diminutive for "squash," but everyone in this country has a mental picture of one type. In England they would be lost among other kinds called "vegetable marrows," and the French word for "squash" is as all-inclusive as our own name for the larger group. Most are not Italian in any sense, since the species, which includes pumpkins, summer crooknecks, and scallops was of American Indian origin, as is the word "squash." In several countries national tastes and skills have developed special lines that have little resemblance in shape or taste; a pumpkin and a scallop squash would not be confused. Among the green summer squashes there is less diversity of form but a great deal of difference in color, taste, and use.

The popular Italian zucchini is called *cocozelle.* It grows long, slim, and striped. The mature fruits have a tendency to curl or twist their necks, which makes them unsuitable for dishes such as stuffed zucchini. *Cocozelle* has a flavor equal to any squash, and if you are thinking of boiling slices or chunks with or without additions of sauces, it is excellent. It is the most vigorous-growing squash, which is why small ones can never be found.

At the other end of the scale are those squashes called *courgettes*, which is the *French* diminutive for "squash." But *courgettes* and zucchini are not the same at all. *Courgettes* should be picked when finger-size and fried whole in olive oil. Their skin is pale green and white striped, much like our 'Greyzini.' When these tiny squashes grow to any size they are no better than and often inferior to other varieties. I have the ones advertised in England as "the true French" and another from the mother country whose name could be translated as "early market." Both are a little pear-shaped, so this year I'm planting one from the south of France called 'Ronde de Nice.' Perhaps the seedsmen of Nice have discovered that it is hard to brown a squash that sits up on its elbows.

The vegetables we buy as zucchini in the market stalls are cylindrical, medium-green to almost black, and sometimes mottled with flecks of white. When freshly picked they are all good. There is also an All American winner called 'Chefini,' an F_1 hybrid, that is better. A similar French hybrid called 'Abondance' (Vilmorin) is at least its equal. These are ideal when small, and if a few get larger than expected in a day or two, the shape makes them ideal for stuffing and baking.

One favorite, if modest, dish that can be made from any of these squashes consists of squash blossoms. There are male and female blooms on the same squash plant (which is a friendly arrangement), but the male produces only the yellow flower. They are easy to tell apart since the female flower will have a tiny beginning squash immediately behind the petals and the male flower is on a long stem. If the male flowers are gathered, dipped in egg batter, and lightly fried in oil, the result is as delectable as it is different.

There are many other kinds of summer squash, and all like a very rich compost and lots of water. The straight-necked yellow squash called 'Butterbar' is very good, but the other new hybrids among the crooknecks and scallops have not lived up to expectations here, so we still grow the standard varieties. Among the winter squashes, which belong to a different species, the very old turban or turk's cap is always a delight for its shape and the variety of colors it displays.

Recipes

The Basic Carrot Dish

12 medium-sized (6 inches long) carrots,
touchon *or other Nantes type*
1 cup rich chicken stock
3 tbs. butter
2 tbs. sugar
salt and pepper
Several sprigs of mint

Slice the carrots lengthwise. Combine stock, butter, and sugar in a shallow casserole or a skillet that can be covered, add carrots, and cook for not over 20 minutes. As the broth is reduced, turn carrots frequently in the thickened sauce. Just before they are done, add a few chopped mint leaves for a touch of savory flavor. Serve in a shallow dish with the slices divided by sprigs of parsley and mint for decoration.

A More Basic Carrot Dish

*15 fingerling carrots, 4 inches long (*sucram *is perfect, but the Dutch 'Amstel' or other small varieties will do)*
1 cup shelled petit pois *('Petit Pois Gullivert' or 'Petit Provençal')*
4 shallots
3 tbs. butter

Cook the carrots whole, without peeling. Slice the shallots, sauté them in butter, and set them aside. When the carrots are tender, slip the skin off by rubbing between thumb and forefinger. Cut into ½-inch pieces. Boil the *petit pois* for 3 minutes in ¼ cup water, drain if necessary, and combine with the carrots. When guests are seated, combine carrots, peas, and shallots and whisk them together over low heat. Place in a covered serving dish, and let them meld for a few moments before serving.

Beets with Greens

(Some beets make better greens and others have more delicate roots, so two varieties are called for if you have them.)

20 'Beet Spinel' (none larger than a ping-pong ball)
Leaves cut from 4 'Crapaudine' (save the large roots for pickled beets another day)
4 tbs. olive oil
1 clove garlic
2 slices bacon, chopped

First boil the tiny 'Beet Spinel' beets unpeeled; when fork-tender set aside. Boil the beet greens in the water left after rinsing plus ½ cup to keep the bottom ones from scorching. Include the bacon; it will add a salty-smoky flavor. Remove and drain greens, pour olive oil into the pot with slices of the garlic, and sauté lightly. Just before serving, combine all ingredients and whisk them together over a low heat.

Curried Turnips

Turnips can be boiled or put in a mutton stew, but that method is for the unsophisticated. To bring out the delicate flavor of the best kinds try them curried.

30 tiny 'Tokyo Cross' turnips, whole (1 inch in diameter), or slices from 4 tender and young standard varieties
1 oz. butter
2 tbs. home-grown and homemade curry powder (see Chapter 7)
1 oz. walnut oil or olive oil (to make an inexpensive walnut oil, mix 1 part real walnut oil to 3 parts peanut oil and let stand over-night; the mixture will have the same nutty flavor)

There are two approaches to this dish. You can sauté the turnips in the oil and butter and sprinkle the curry as the turnips become tender and are turned in the pan. The result will be a turnip slice or ball served with a visible covering of the curry.

Or you can add the curry directly to the oil and butter while it is heating. Sprinkle on a little more curry as the turnips frizzle to a tender brown in the skillet.

Summer Squash: *Avacodella* or Argentine marrow

1 squash 6 inches in diameter
1 clove pink garlic
3 tbs. olive oil
2 tsp. fresh summer savory and thyme minced

Cut squash in half, but don't peel. Parboil 10 to 15 minutes or until tender. Remove outside rind, which will leave the dark-green outer surface and a light-green inner one. Cut these into wedges as you would an avocado, and then lightly sauté in the oil, garlic, and herbs. If you want more color and zing, add yellow wax peppers and, at the last moment, pimientos.

Zucchini Casserole

6 medium zucchini (to 8 inches long; our 'Chefini' and the French 'Abondance' are firm and ideal)
1 large red Spanish or bottle onion
3 large tomatoes
Monterey jack cheese
Basil and oregano
Salt and pepper

Cut the zucchini lengthwise in ¼-inch strips; cut the onions into thin slices. Gently sauté the onion slices in olive oil until tender and clear (5 to 7 minutes). Next lightly brown the zucchini strips in the same oil, turning several times. Cut the cheese into ¼-inch ribbons, and slice the tomatoes as you would for salads. In the bottom of the casserole place a layer of zucchini, then onion slices, next the tomatoes, and top with a few ribbons of cheese. Salt and pepper, and add a sprinkling of finely chopped basil and oregano. Continue the same process until three or four levels have built up in the casserole. Bake uncovered in a preheated oven at 350° for 10 to 15 minutes, until the whole has melted together.

Stuffed Zucchini

4 zucchini to 10 inches long
1 onion, chopped
½ cup diced prosciutto, salami, or ham
¼ cup bread crumbs
¼ cup diced cheese
1 egg
1 clove garlic
Basil and marjoram
4 tbs. olive oil

Trim stem end and parboil whole squash 3 minutes. Drain and cut in half lengthwise. Scoop out the pulp and save in mixing bowl. Fry the chopped onions in olive oil until tender, then add crushed garlic, finely chopped basil, and marjoram and sauté onions 4 minutes longer. Then add mixture to the zucchini pulp along with the egg, prosciutto, and cheese. Gently stir these ingredients together. Place the zucchini halves on an oiled baking pan and fill each hull with the mixture, then top it with bread crumbs and a sprinkling of grated cheese. Bake in a preheated oven at 350° for 15 to 25 minutes, depending upon the size of the squash.

1/6
Broad Bean
HARIÇOT
Flageolet blanc
longue cosse
Vilmorin
COU
Abondance
35¢
CRESS
GARDEN
MANDEVILLE
SEEDS
kwiek

4 Staples: Beans, Peas, and Tomatoes

Beans, peas, and tomatoes are the vegetables that do so much for spring and summer meals. It is often pleasant just to eat them raw in the garden as a kind of appetizer or refreshment. Luckily, they also dry, freeze, and can, so keeping a year-round supply is easy. A few standard varieties of these vegetables supply most commercial markets, whether canned, frozen, or fresh. But for the home gardener there are endless varieties; I have always had a waiting list of kinds to try.

THE BEAN SCENE

It is a tribute to the high place various beans hold in most cultures that the word "bean" can mean so many different kinds of things. For example, the broadbean of the Old World is used here only as a cover crop to provide nitrogen for the soil. Often it is referred to contemptuously as a "horse bean." But in Europe many types of broadbean have been developed as choice table varieties, and they are found in several of the recipes in the *Escoffier Cook Book* (Crown Publishers).

On the other hand, lima beans are something of an American specialty, at least when eaten green out of the shell, and soya beans of the East come in so many varieties that you can't begin to explore them. (Some soya beans are not edible, but others are most delicate.) The black beans of Mexico have a little of the mushroom in their flavor and stand quite apart from other beans.

Several times I have tried to put in some logical order all the common beans listed in French and English seed catalogs, garden books, and dictionaries. I can't, so I'll make only three distinctions: green beans, which are intended to be eaten pod and all; flageolets, in which the seed can be eaten green to advantage (but not the pods); and the various dry beans. All the 500 or more varieties of dry bean belong to the single species *Phaseolus vulgaris.*

Green Beans. These may be called stringbeans, snap beans, or French beans. Some grow on poles and trellises, and others are stiff-stemmed plants that need no support. There is also a group somewhere in between called "half runner." Generally, the dwarf varieties tend to be hardier and can be planted earlier and therefore bear sooner. (That first gathering of tiny pods will practically make a meal no matter what else is served.)

Last year, pushing luck, I planted six varieties of beans at the end of February, which is at least a month too early even here in northern California, but how else can you learn? The pole beans were wiped out entirely, and the dwarf types came up with such straggling rows that they had to be replanted. The purple-podded 'Royalty' stood up well. Mind you I was covering all these with flower pots every frosty night. The pods from 'Royalty' were less than I expected, but that may have been caused by the climate.

My early spring garden. (Joyce R. Wilson photo)

'Phenix Claudia' beans. (J. Williamson photo)

The best for both hardiness and perfection of taste was 'Phenix Claudia' (in English catalogs this is sometimes listed as 'Phenis Claudia,' which is the French pronunciation). The seeds are new-moon-shaped and a rich purple. It is completely stringless from youth to maturity, which is more than can be said for such famous ones as 'Fin de Bagnols' and 'Triomphe de Farcy.' The latter's name suggests that the idea of the "French-cut" bean was devised to remedy their defects.

The All America Award winner called 'Executive' is another outstanding dwarf. It too is stringless and resists heat. Green beans dislike hot, dry weather, and if it is windy as well, their blossoms will fail to set until conditions are more to their liking. This variety, which I planted at the end of May, was still producing enough for the table in mid-October, and of the best quality right along.

Some French beans have either a yellow or a purple pod. The purple one is something of a loss

Pimientos on the bush. Any dish of green beans is improved in taste and color by strips of pimiento that have been roasted in olive oil. (Matt Barr photo)

since it turns green while cooking; yellow pods retain much of their color, which is very nice if you have different varieties and are thinking of serving a cold platter. An oval white platter lined with green beans that have been cooked to keep their color, a few yellow kinds, and a few strips of pimento for red accent will be the feature of any table setting.

The favorite yellow variety in both England and France is 'Mont d'or,' to which the English have added the redundant 'Golden Butter' in case you have missed the point. Burpee's 'Brittle Wax' is a good substitute. Remember that none of the yellow-podded varieties will equal the best green ones for flavor — it's the color that you're after.

Pole Beans. The term "runner beans" sounds more elegant than "pole beans," but the former is likely to be confused with the 'Scarlet Runners,' which are different, although many are edible. To most Americans, the pole beans are divided between the 'Kentucky Wonder' and the 'Blue Lake' varieties; 'Kentucky Wonder' is preferred in the East and 'Blue Lake' in the West. However, I find that people who move around carry their preferences with them, so preference is probably not a matter of geographical area.

There are many other pole beans and some are better, so the home gardener should not limit himself. All varieties like a well-worked soil, rich in manure or compost, and some shade around their scrawny ankles. Peppers and many of the bushier herbs that like to sop up as much sun as possible are good shade providers for pole beans. The bamboo trellis is better than a teepee of poles or a single pole in climates where you are likely to get a few blazing days. It provides some shade for a number of plants and blossoms.

Green beans only? Well, perhaps also purple. One of the most famous is the French 'Blue Coco,' which is close to the 'Blue Queen' (Suttons). Both are choice for flavor (although the color has nothing to do with flavor). Like 'Royalty' these purple beans turn green when cooked. The contrast of green and purple mingled on the vine is most attractive, and on the practical side, it allows the gardener to find and pick them while they are still small.

'Romano' is the flat, larged-seeded bean that is popular in the frozen-food departments of stores. Its flavor may not be as delicate as that of some other green beans, but it is different — a little crunchier perhaps. For the hearty Italian soup of mixed vegetables called minestrone, it is perfect. Any large seeds of 'Romano' that have become mature can be shelled and added for that in-between quality which is different from either green or dry savor and texture.

There are always some surprises for a gardener who tries everything at least once. Nichols had a contest to find family-preserved varieties of beans; a Mrs. Rickles of Alabama turned up a black-seeded pole bean that supposedly originated in Ireland. These beans are good enough for a permanent place in your garden.

'Blue Queen,' a British pole bean that rivals 'Blue Coco' in quality. (Matt Barr photo)

Flageolets. Flageolets are not widely grown here, but they are most rewarding. If planted in good soil after the weather has come around, they grow just as well as any other dwarf French bean, although their production is much less, which may be why they are seldom grown in this country, where we ask for a bowlful rather than a spoonful. (The same reasoning accounts for our prejudice against dry beans.)

Flageolets can be shelled like green peas and cooked in the immature state. For that purpose 'Vert Suma' (Nichols) is the best flageolet. The season for the fresh ones is, of course, very short, even with several plantings. Most recipes calling for flageolets refer to the dry but not quite mature seeds that maintain their green coloring. 'Roi des Vert' is standard and superb; almost identical is one called 'Flageolet Chevrier.' I mention it because you can buy the seeds from a New Jersey importer.

Americanized French cookbooks say that any white bean can be substituted for flageolets, which of course is absurd. A potato can be substituted for rice, since both are starches, but it would boggle most rice dishes. Even Escoffier suggests that the seed of other dwarf French beans can be substituted. But since the little jade-and-white seeds of flageolets have a delicacy that surprises anyone who has never tasted them, why not have the real thing that will always please your guests.

Cassoulet dishes are the most famous use for flageolets; these are often made to serve with lamb or sausages. (I often use a simple version, not in the proportions found in most recipes.) Do not soak flageolets in water overnight or cook them in it, for water is the enemy of good cooking. Take a quart of chicken broth rich enough to be jellied, or better yet, a mixture of ham and chicken broth. Add about ½ cup of flageolets, and bring them to a boil for 4 minutes. This amount of beans sounds small, but it will be about right to absorb most of the broth in the final cooking.

This first step can be done the night before or early in the morning. Then set aside the mixture. The second cooking, during dinner preparation, will take about an hour, or until the flageolets are tender and most but not all of the broth has been absorbed by them. Toward serving time, simmer sausages in apple juice until the juice has evaporated and the sausages have browned. Combine them with the flageolets and a small amount of enriched broth. No one will get more than a few serving spoonfuls of the dish, but it is so rich that no more is needed.

Coco Beans. Coco beans can be treated much like the flageolet. The dry seed is roundish, about the size of an English pea, and when in the "green" stage these beans are most delectable. They are more abundant in production and easier to shell than the flageolets, so for that reason alone they are worth a row. The one I use is called 'Chinese Yellow' in English catalogs or 'Coco Jaune de la Chine' in the French ones. There are also white and pink versions, but I have not tried them.

Broad Beans. These too can be eaten in either the green or the dry state. They are flat in a rumpled way and larger than a thumbnail. They are called *feves* in France, *fava* in Italy, and *Fabra* by the botanist. They are a slow-growing, cool-weather crop that will withstand moderate but not great cold. Broad beans are popular in England but are not much developed here; we grow the edible varieties as much for their nitrogen-producing qualities as for the beans.

'Aquadulce Claudia' has proved to be the best broad bean for California. It can be planted in October and grows vigorously through the winter for an early spring crop. 'Green Longpod' (Suttons) does well if planted in late winter or early spring. These *fava* beans do have a use to the gourmet cook: a purée of them works in East Indian dishes that call for *pulses*, and they are excellent as the thickening ingredient in minestrone. The seeds, whether green or dry, have to be boiled and peeled in order to remove the hard outer shell and thin inner one.The shells have to be discarded like the shell of a walnut or the layers around a chestnut.

The inner meat has a flavor good enough to stand by itself if the peeled beans are cooked in butter to which chopped marjoram and savory have been added. Served alone, they are a little heavy for most menus and not a few stomachs. Again, the best procedure is to serve only a tiny side dish. If the dinner is well planned, there will be no need to suggest that only a spoonful is needed.

Dry Beans. There is no need to grow most of the familiar dry beans in a home garden unless you're hungry and thinking of saving kitchen costs. The common kinds are all harvested when fully ripe, so there is no edge there, and the space used is better devoted to rarer things. However, there is one exception: a French variety that is not available here, so the only possibility is to grow it: 'Comtesse de Chambord.' It is a small round white bean of superb flavor. In production it is between the flageolets and the common beans, and it can be used in place of either. The flavor is not equal to that of the flageolet, but it is far ahead of the various navy beans because it has a lightness in both flavor and effect. The Countess, by the way, was a mid-nineteenth-century patroness of both flowers and vegetables. If she had had a choice, she probably would have wanted to have her name immortalized by a bloom rather than a bean, but at least the fame of her name will last for many years.

Ordinary kidney beans should not be neglected by the gourmet. If the red one is combined with chick-peas and the oriental black bean or the Mexican black bean, a salad of color and taste can be set on the table. Mix the several beans with olive oil, anchovies, and a few fine herbs, and stir occasionally until the flavors blend. Before serving, lay down a bed of home-grown lettuce in several varieties, and mix the beans with a small can of tuna fish. That is a picnic meal in itself.

PEAS

Probably you have bought a frozen packet labeled *petit pois* or have seen them listed on a restaurant menu. This is a fair literal translation, since it only means "little peas." In a canning or freezing process it is very easy to screen out the larger and older peas; the smaller ones left are certain to be more tender, but they are not the true thing. *Petit pois* are a group of varieties bred never to grow larger than a smidgen. They have no bulk or weight and are thus strictly for the home gardener.

English catalogs list 'Petit Pois Gullivert' as the true French variety. This is a recently patented introduction, however, and no truer than the former name of 'Petit Provençal.' 'Gullivert' grows about 18 inches tall for me, requires no staking, stands the winter better than others, and is the first to bear. These virtues, plus its superb flavor, compensate for the fact that the yield of tiny peas is never enough, which is why recipes often call for filling out a dish with small onions or some of the fingerling carrots mentioned in Chapter 3.

Snow Peas. These are the edible pod peas or *mangetout*; some are found in markets. They are essential in certain oriental dishes, blending perfectly with water chestnuts. There are several kinds, but none is better than 'Carouby de Maussane.' (The first part of the name refers to the pod of a carob tree, which they do resemble.) Since the young pods are good enough to eat right off the vine, little cooking is necessary.

'Carouby' has to be given a support because it

grows to about 5 feet in height. Unlike *petit pois*, which have pure-white blossoms, 'Carouby' has purple and lavender petals. Another variety with similar blooms is called 'Purple Podded' (Suttons); it is not a *mangetout* or edible-pod variety but is an attractive shelling pea. Its seeds are green, so it differs from 'Carouby' in that its vine is ornamental.

Standard Peas. There is surprising agreement on the more productive peas. 'Little Marvel' is listed in both English and American catalogs, while its improved form, 'Kelvedon Wonder,' is sold in France under the name 'Merveille de Kelvedon.' One American variety should be mentioned because of its season: 'Wando.' It has been listed for a long time, but many people don't realize that unlike most peas, this one will bear in the full heat of summer.

Peas need little nitrogen since they produce it for themselves, but they do need phosphorus and potash, so I add bonemeal and a liberal amount of wood ashes (from the fireplace) during the season in which peas thrive.

TOMATOES

If the New World hadn't introduced tomatoes, cookbooks from many countries would be very different. Potatoes and yams may be more important in terms of keeping people alive, but not in terms of shaping menus. Tomatoes are so basic that most gardeners have a conservative tendency.

American tomato varieties vary from good to superb, if grown in a rich soil with enough heat. In France and England, the climate is not favorable for our kinds, so they have developed medium and small types that will mature with less heat. They are nothing like the great rich slices the good American varieties will produce, but they might have a place in the coastal regions of California, Oregon, and Washington, or anywhere else with a short season.

(Opposite) Roasting peppers such as 'Anaheim' are piquant but not really hot. Either fresh or home-canned, they are perfect chopped into tomato sauces.

The European tomato that has proved itself is the Scottish-developed 'Tangella.' It was designed as a greenhouse plant for winter or a cold climate. Outside it also does well no matter what the climate, and its small orange fruits are useful when November comes around and the mists arrive. Most of these small varieties, which were developed for low temperature, fail because the skins will rupture in warm weather and mold will set in. Last year I composted an entire crop of 'Seaford Abundance' for that reason.

I am a conservative radical when it comes to growing tomatoes — radical because each year I try new kinds. 'Spring Giant,' which recently won the All America Award, is now part of my holy trinity. On the conservative side, nothing has turned up here that is better than 'Big Boy' (for me, of course). Others, like beefsteak, are thicker; 'San Marzano' is even thicker but is good only for tomato paste.

The nonacidic 'Jubilee' is without a peer among the "yellow" tomatoes. ('Tangella' has the color but is even more acid than our standard tomatoes.) Blandness can be a good thing, and the juxtaposition of the red with acid and the yellow without acid will set up a contrast of sense impressions that has to be seen and tasted.

Recipes

Peas with Mushrooms

1 cup peas
½ lb. fresh champignons
8 to 10 cocktail onions (Sutton's has a good one, but even onion sets will do or slices of 'White Lisbon')
1 small heart butterhead lettuce
2 tbs. butter
2 tbs. olive oil

Mix peas, onions, and oil and let stand. Wilt mushrooms (quartered or sliced in butter). Then wilt the lettuce heart in the same skillet. Add peas and onions to this with enough stock (3 tbs.) to keep the combination moist while simmering for 5 minutes or less. Since both peas and lettuce are good raw, the time is a matter of choice.

Creamed Peas

There are recipes for "mature," i.e. overripe, peas that call for a cream sauce. For a very light luncheon with only a clear soup and green salad, this might be in order:

1 cup peas
1 egg
2 tbs. butter
1 tsp. flour
4 tbs. salami or prosciutto, finely chopped
¾ cup milk

Add milk and flour to melted butter and stir until smooth, then whip in egg. Place peas and diced meat in double boiler, cover with sauce, and simmer 20 minutes.

Green (Unripe) Flageolets

1 cup shelled flageolets ('Roi de Vert,' 'Vert Summa,' or the white flageolet 'Blanca longue cosse')
5 shallots (diced silverskin onions will also do)
¼ cup water

Simmer the beans for 12 to 15 minutes — no longer or the nutty flavor will go. Fry shallots in oil, and add the bean seeds, mixing them together for a few moments. If they are to be served with a meat dish like roast lamb, spoon them into the bottom of the serving platter where they will pick up all the flavors of the meat juices. Needless to say, each guest gets only a spoonful of this delicacy, but aahhhh!

Cassoulet

½ cup dry flageolet beans
1 qt. chicken broth (or 1 pt. chicken and 1 pt. ham broth)
12 sausages
8 oz. apple juice

Never soak beans overnight in water! Cook them in the broth for 4 minutes, and set aside overnight or at least for a day. During that time the two flavors will have a long conversation and come to an agreement. Final cooking of beans and broth will take about 1 hour. While the mixture is cooking, begin to simmer the sausages in apple juice. When the liquid has disappeared, the sausages will begin to brown. When flageolets and sausage have integrated, they are combined in the residual juices.

Green Beans as a Cold Dish

2 lbs. snap beans ('Phenix Claudia,' 'Executive,' etc.)
6 quarts salted water
Pimientos, canned or roasted
Salt and pepper
Olive oil

To keep the bright-green color, bring the salted water to a boil; then sprinkle the beans into the water in several handfuls so that the water doesn't stop boiling. Cook for 7 minutes. (If it requires 10 or 15 minutes to make them tender, you have either the wrong age or the wrong variety.) Drain beans and immediately immerse them in a large pot of water to which ice cubes have been added. You must chill them immediately, even if you need more than one pot of ice water.

Drain beans again, place on a platter, and spoon 3 tbs. of olive oil over them. Keep in refrigerator until serving time, then interlace with strips of roasted pimientos, and add a few sprinkles of wine vinegar (if this is put on earlier, it leaches out some of the green color). Freshly roasted peppers are the best, but these are usually not available until fall, whereas early green beans are the best. Hence we compromise with the thinner variety early in the season.

Tomato Salsa

2 tomatoes at their peak
1 cucumber
2 green peppers (sweet)
1 yellow 'Hungarian Wax' pepper
1 Spanish onion
3 tbs. olive oil
Garlic (optional)
Vinegar

Slice all ingredients in ½-inch chunks (or a little larger for the tomatoes). Mix them together in the oil and vinegar, and allow the combination to sit for at least an hour before serving.

There are versions called *salsa borracha*, or "drunken sauce." Most consist of adding more peppers, either dried and ground or fresh, perhaps with wine or liquor taking the place of vinegar. It is believed that the hot peppers will add a blow strong enough to cure the previous night's tipplers of any shadows left in their mind's web.

Plain Tomato

The best thing to do with a tomato is almost nothing; for which, take:

2 large red tomatoes
1 yellow tomato (such as 'Jubilee' or its versions)
4 sprigs dill at the 6-inch stage

Save the juice, because the acid of the red and the blandness of the yellow will run together. Peel and slice each, arranging them on a large platter in a single layer. Chop dill weed (leaves) over all these, spot each with olive oil, and let stand for at least an hour before serving. The platter can either be left at room temperature or chilled before serving.

Stuffed Tomatoes

One should not forget that tomatoes are not only delicious for themselves but excellent vehicles for seafoods.

6 to 8 very large tomatoes ('Big Boy' and 'Spring Giant' are ideal)
Salt, pepper, oil
2 cups fresh shrimp (or shelled crab, anchovies, or tuna)
Basil or tarragon

Peel the tomatoes and cut them in half. Scoop out enough seeds to make a hollow, then turn the halves upside down on paper towel and let the juices drain out. I prefer to just salt and pepper the cavity, line it with chopped basil or tarragon, and fill it with precooked shrimp or crab with green mayonnaise. Tuna fish is a rather easy out and will do when shrimp and crab are out of season.

This is a salad-cocktail to be served in a rosette of escarolle or lettuce. However, if you like the tomatoes cooked, fry the hollow halves open side down in hot oil for 3 minutes. Next fill with a mix of bread crumbs browned in butter, a squeeze of garlic, and either grated anchovies or crumbled tuna in which chopped herbs have been mixed. Fill the tomato hulls and bake in a 375° oven for 10 to 15 minutes.

5 Greens

The most adaptable vegetables are the green ones. Think of water cress that is delightful in salads, but when lightly cooked in chicken broth makes a memorable soup. Many greens can be boiled, yet few of them are not equally good just as they are, seasoned with a little olive oil and perhaps some of the delicate herbs.

There are vegetables that are intensely or delicately green in taste, but not necessarily green in their leaf color. There are some whose leaves are on the golden-yellow side, a few that feather their greens with reds and purples, some that are reddish-purple, and still others that have a silvery cast or patina on the leaves. These color combinations may not correspond with the different tastes, but they do provide for handsome color arrangements when a table is set.

Grain products and meats are the basic diet for most people, but the addition of greens improves a meal. Since many meats have a distinct flavor (game for example, is lean and dry in texture), the lush and delicate leaves of herbaceous plants in early growth impart a mild, spicy, or tart accent to any dinner depending on what variety you use. So a dinner consisting of only rare roast beef and a large green salad (with perhaps a few slices of French bread, to take advantage of the drippings) will provide modest perfection.

Good green salads are always made by combinations. For a little tartness try the many chicories or upland cress, and for a slight acid touch the sorrels are far ahead of the usual squeeze of lemon. These acid leaves distribute evenly throughout the salad, yet provide a green to bite into and raise the question of combined flavors. As a base, there are always the blander varieties of lettuce, but they vary greatly in texture. Crispness or softness is a different concept from taste or color, but it influences what the palate registers.

In early spring a salad can be made entirely of seasonal greens: the youngest of mustard leaves, a few from *scarole* (a French chicory), and the peppery Miners lettuce, which is a wildling here. Later in the season there are all kinds of lettuce, then artichoke hearts, and finally the red and gold slices of tomatoes in midsummer.

For the simplest of green salads, dressings should never be poured over the leaves — it turns them limp and disguises many of the tenderest flavors of combined greens. Place a few tablespoons of olive oil (3 or 4 to my taste) in the bottom of a wooden bowl. Add 2 tablespoons of the best white-wine vinegar you can afford, then a little salt, and a clove of garlic sliced. Next add freshly chopped herbs like tarragon, thyme, and sweet marjoram to the base and macerate together with a wooden spoon.

This preparation can begin well ahead of time because the oil and vinegar will extract the combination of flavors. The various greens can be put over the oil and herb dressing if it is not too soon before dinnertime, but they shouldn't be tossed until just before serving. Lettuce will provide the major portion of the salad, although in spring, when their flavor is bland, some of the chicories can make up a third of the salad. You should only use a few leaves of sorrels and mustard greens.

LETTUCE

You can certainly make a green salad using ordinary head lettuce, but it is better for a restaurant-type salad. The crisp leaves of heading lettuces are tasty and will stand up under a drenching of French or blue-cheese salad dressings, but when used that way they are then merely serving as the medium to convey the flavor of the dressing, which is not the real thing.

The semi-heading, loose-leaf lettuces are the best for the base of an elaborate green salad. The 'Bibb' has the highest reputation for succulence and flavor; in Europe there are a number of quite similar varieties. However, the very delicacy of 'Bibb' lettuce can be a drawback for the home gardener. A market gardener can sell his entire crop in one cutting once the heads have reached perfection, but the home gardener needs only a head or two at a time. When a row or two of 'Bibb' lettuces are left in the ground, the tenderness that is their glory make them vulnerable. Bad weathering is a gardening constant; in long periods of rainy or damp days the delicate leaves may rot inwardly. Have a succession of very short rows, or even better, work little clusters of eight to ten heads into odd corners or into the flower garden. Lettuce is a cool-weather crop, and as the season grows warm, it appreciates the shade of ornamental shrubbery.

Some catalogs list 'Bibb' as a heading lettuce, but that conveys the wrong impression. It makes a little rosette, something like the stone chalcedony. Other catalogs call them butterheads, which is a better suggestion since it doesn't suggest the globular cabbage head. An understudy is butter-crunch, and it will stand both more heat and more rain than 'Bibb.'

For truly looseleaf lettuces, the standard American varieties, such as 'Prizehead,' 'Oak leaf,' and 'Salad Bowl' are hard to beat if they are well grown — that is, unless one gets into winter and forcing lettuce. For me, 'Oak Leaf' lasts after the others have bolted, but I always try to mix planting so that bolting is no problem.

There is a recent introduction called 'Salad Trim.' (It deservedly won an All America Award.) The leaves in early season look like cordovan leather, and the outside ones are only a little more tender. Since deep purple has always had an appeal to me, I grew a few more rounds. After all, a pink salmon served on a bedding of purple lettuce is a visual treat.

My opinion is that 'Salad Trim' must be derived from the 'Cos' or 'Romaine' lettuce, since it is very frost-hardy and has the same candle-flame-shaped head as 'Romaine.' The inner cluster of leaves seems superior to the standard varieties, even if you aren't thinking of its decorative touch. Like other 'Cos' varieties, it is even crisper than standard heading lettuce. Whoever thought of the "trim" in its name doubtless had the right concept for its use, but beyond that, a few of these purple leaves in a green salad add more than decoration.

There is a standard English variety that should also be tried: 'Webbs Wonderful.' There they call it a "cabbage-type," which means that it forms some kind of a head if left that long. The head is not

nearly as compact as "cabbage" would imply, and, if picked early, it will be much like a curly-leaved 'Butterhead.' I am attached to it because last year, when the temperature reached 101°, 'Webbs Wonderful' kept its arms folded while many others bolted.

WINTER GREENS

Winter Lettuce. There is a lettuce of possibly French origin that does well in winter. Seed can be bought in this country under the name 'Marvel of Besson.' Its use is indicated in the French name, *mervaille de quatre saisons*, but something that will do well in all four seasons anywhere is a fantasy, of course. Some plants will tolerate a variety of soil and air temperatures, but all have a preference.

The marvel of this variety is that although it is nothing special in summer, it is very winter-hardy. In mornings it might be limp with frost, but it keeps on growing as though this were routine. There are standard winter lettuce varieties that will do well in the South and West, where the climate is not continuously cold. 'Romaine' will notably do better than the loose or semiheading types if subjected to days of frost.

Midwinter brings the short days and the dim sun. For many vegetables this won't do at all, but some greens, including lettuce, are more tender if sheltered from the sun. It is the same principle as blanching celery. Although little light may be needed for these lettuces, heat definitely is. This may mean cold frames, hot beds, or a greenhouse. The home gardener may only require a porch.

There are varieties that have been developed for the short time of year. They will have to be forced in cold regions but will survive outside where frost is only an occasional problem. Two varieties are Dutch, one called 'Kweik' and the other 'Kordaat.' The latter has my vote since here it grows neck and

(Opposite) This American lettuce is nearly purple; it is colorful in salads and makes a splendid garnish for other dishes. (Joyce R. Wilson photo)

(Opposite)'Marvel of Besson'is a bronze-leafed semi-heading lettuce from France that is suited to all four seasons. (Joyce R. Wilson photo)

neck with escarole when planted outside in November or December. 'Kweik' is more modest, even if its name does mean "quick."

It is not necessary to send to Holland to get this seed. Both major seedsmen in Britain sell packets that are bred and then sealed by the Dutch. These Dutch varieties have to be forced under glass. The French also have several varieties that have to be grown this way. (Forcing is a difficult proposition for the amateur unless he can be around the garden and the frames all day long.) 'D'hiver de Verrieres' is a Vilmorin introduction. For the most part, winter lettuce is something that serves to prolong the summer or to shorten the winter. Thus another variety is called, pleasantly, 'Suzan' (Vilmorin). In climates milder than northern France it does very well in midwinter. The catalogs refer to it as a blond type, which probably speaks for itself — a light-colored head. It is much like 'Bibb,' except that the leaves are a little thicker and hardier.

Other Winter Salad Greens. Midwinter may be the time to settle for greens imported from milder climates. During this season you might even use the basic lettuce from stores or the greens better suited to winter. Mustard greens, sorrels, the various chicories, and wildlings such as lamb's lettuce are all midwinter growers. Where snow covers the ground until late in the season that will be no help, but sorrel can be grown indoors anywhere and several kinds of chicory can too.

By themselves, all these greens are too dominant for a salad, but they can be used as cooked greens (pot herbs as these are sometimes called) or in soups.

Sorrel. Of the winter greens, sorrel is one of the most accommodating. It is perennial and will grow equally well in a pot or tub or in any corner of the garden. Only a few leaves will transform dull store-bought lettuce into something special. And a few more leaves from the same pot or tub make a superb soup or omelet.

Sorrel has a leaf like an Indian arrowhead and roots like tiny parsnips. These roots keep splitting to send out more leaves until the clump gets so compact that it needs dividing. These divisions can be made over and over without any loss of flavor. One set of the variety 'White Chambourcy' has been with me since 1946, when I got the seeds from the Indiana Botanic Garden. It has moved from house to house four times since, and has been divided, shared, and set here and there in the garden more times than I can count.

Sorrels do have their troubles. Snails and rabbits, as well as guests, love it. In a pot or tub these problems are easy to control. The variety one can buy on a seed rack in this country is 'Bellville,' and my favored 'White Chambourcy' (Vilmorin) is only an improved version of it. The latter has thinner, paler, and more delicately flavored leaves. It can be ordered from French seed firms, who also carry another variety of merit that was originally called 'Blonde de Lyon.' It is now likely to be listed as 'Improved Blonde' or some such. The leaves are much rounder. For those who wish to order from France, remember that the French word for sorrel is *oseille.*

Sorrels prefer an acid soil, but that doesn't seem to be the reason for their acid flavor. The acidity of the leaf is dependent on the amount of sunlight they receive. When the sun is weak in winter, the flavor is bland. In summer I try to keep my plantings of divisions in shady spots, since I like sorrel understated rather than clamoring.

'Suzan' is another good French variety of winter lettuce. (Joyce R. Wilson photo)

Winter salad bed: Dutch lettuce in front, chicory and sorrel with multiplying onions and parsley at rear. (Joyce R. Wilson photo)

For use in salads, soups, or omelets, remove the mid-rib from several leaves, and fold the tender part into a spool. When this is sliced crosswise, the result is a few delicate ribbons that can be added directly to a green salad.

For those who are unfamiliar with the taste of sorrel, sorrel soup is a good introduction. The simplest method of preparation is to wilt the sorrel ribbons in butter and then pour a very rich chicken broth over them. This seems fine and simple to me, but the true gourmet will probably add three egg yolks whipped into a cup of cream to the simmering broth and sorrel. The result is certainly richer and thicker, and if it is all you are having for lunch on a cold winter day, it will make a meal in itself, assuming that there are a few slices of garlic bread to dip into it.

Chicory. All the many kinds of chicory have a bitter taste as opposed to the acids of sorrel. They are not even distantly related, since chicory belongs to the daisy family, but their leaves do combine well in a salad. A few kinds of chicory are also most beautiful. There is a narrow-leaved sort that the Italians call *radicchio*; it should be grown for its wonderful sky-blue ray flowers. These blooms open in foggy dawns or toward sunset but don't like midday.

Radicchio is useful for making *barbé,* a pot herb. Pull up the saw-toothed leaves and the white roots and cook them together. It is wise to boil the roots and leaves in two waters to reduce the bitterness. The result is basic to some Italian menus.

Another variety that should be avoided for salad greens is called 'Magdeburg.' Its roots are dried and ground to make a coffee substitute or additive; they are used in French Market and other New Orleans coffees. The resulting flavor is like that of the Italian and French double-roasted coffees, in which the same bitterness and blackness is achieved by slightly burning the coffee berries.

The French classify chicories under four headings, and with a bit of overlap that will do here too. The English, as always, have an odd man out, but it happens to be a good one in the salad bowl and as a pot herb. The French categories consist of:

'Chicorées sauvage' ("Wild Chicory"). These are no more wild than any of the others that might be put into a salad. Some are semi-heading.

'Chicorées scarole.' These are often listed by American seedsmen as escarolle. It, too, makes something of a head, but along the lines of a 'Bibb' lettuce.

'Chicorées frisées.' In any good market you will find these often labeled as "endive." There is a really frizzy one and another that is more broad-leaved. Any of the many varieties are good winter greens, but they don't have much meat on their bones.

'Chicorées de Bruxelles.' In American catalogs, this is likely to be listed as either 'Whitloof' or Belgian (Brussels) endive. It is so peculiar and so important that part of a later chapter will be devoted to it.

The frizzled chicory is a sort of garnish, but the inside leaves are most bland and will fill out a midwinter salad. 'Green Curled' (Burpee, etc.) is an American version that seems about as good as any of the European imports (but there are another dozen French varieties that I want to try).

Scarole is more important in a home garden or greenhouse, since it does provide bulk for midwinter greens, or early-spring greens where

(Opposite) Greens for winter salads. At far left is whitloof, or Belgian endive, and at upper left is the same plant before being cut back and forced. All the other plants are chicories: top center, red-leaved chicory; top right, chicory 'Sauvage'; bottom left, chicory frisée (often called endive); bottom right, chicory escarole.

the climate is severe. My neighbors refer to it as "winter lettuce." It is crisp like 'Romaine' and will stand frost down to 20°. It will not grow well in freezing weather, but it will survive and come back again. For midwinter the seed should be sown in August and the seedlings set out well before the first frost so that they will be growing vigorously when the first blows of winter strike.

Scarole responds to light much like sorrel. That is, the more light, the more bitter flavor develops. To lessen this, hill the plants with earth, or mound up straw or sawdust around them. Winter varieties that make a head will, in effect, blanch themselves if you tie up the outer leaves and then discard them, saving only the tender heart. 'En Coronet d'Anjou' is a very good winter-heading variety for milder climates. If you have extra flowerpots of large enough size, set them over the plants.

The English variety 'Sugar Loaf' (Thompson & Morgan) may belong here or with the wild chicories. It makes a large, dense head, looking much like Chinese cabbage. When tender it is perfect for adding to salads, and when fully grown it makes a pot herb. Like many chicories, the root can be dug when the top is cut and replanted in late summer. The root will then send up several clusters of leaves in midwinter. These don't make tender heads, but the leaves are most welcome at that time of year.

The wild chicories are not as bland as *scarole*, but they make a superb garnish if picked young, and in time some produce a mild heart. The two that have served me best for winter salads in late January and early February are both French. (I might point out that our temperature dips into the low 20s and doesn't bother them at all.) The one that Vilmoran calls 'Improved Blonde' is apple-green on the outside leaves, which are round, and in time it produces a nearly white heart.

The young outside leaves can be plucked off a few at a time for early use without disturbing the growth of the later heart.

There are two varieties of wild chicory that have considerable streaks of purple-red patches, which is good for trim. The older one is called 'Rossa di Verona,' which is often translated in French listings as 'Rouge de Verone.' It has a recent cousin that I believe originated in southern France, since the original packets came from there and Vilmorin released it last year in a plain container. It is called 'Rouge de Trevise' and has performed very well for me.

Once the chicory is established, its roots can be dug and planted in a cellar to produce very delicate winter greens that will grow in the dark. The same is true of other chicories and also of the edible dandelion, but these methods will be discussed later under 'Whitloof' or 'Belgian endive.' A happy thing about the whole chicory group is that they can easily be transplanted — the opposite of the parsley family, which often has similar roots but no inclination to move.

There are a few other winter greens that should be mentioned. One of them is the familiar and often hated dandelion. The leaves of even the common kinds are edible, but there are a number of garden varieties that have been developed in southern Europe. One of the pleasures of San Francisco's North Beach, an Italian enclave in a multiracial and multigastronomic paradise, is street vendors selling little tufts of dandelion leaves that are very small-leaved in form and thoroughly bitter. No vendor carries more than a few twists. They are sold by old

(Opposite) Escarole if one is French, *scarole* if one is Italian. (Joyce R. Wilson photo)

Winter salad bed: chicory 'Trevise' on right, escarole in center, and chicory 'Sauvage' at left. (Joyce R. Wilson photo)

men; the object is probably to discuss the garden and the weather with both strangers and compatriots. The lowly dandelion has improved so much that you can now grow cabbage-leaved types that have immense leaves. One or two leaves can be added to a green salad, but generally they are pot greens, and even then the water should be changed several times to reduce bitterness.

Another winter green not grown as much as it should be in this country is called corn salad or lamb's lettuce. In French it is called *mache*, and a number of horticultural varieties have been developed there. *Mache* is used as salad greens in winter and also in a number of cheese dishes.

Minor Pot Herbs. Poke is a somewhat regional pot herb with a popularity mainly in the South, where it is gathered wild. It grows all too well in the garden, even in unfavorable soil, and will in time send up a large, red-stemmed plant with purple berries that are somewhat toxic to birds and probably to humans. For cooking, only the first clusters of leaves that come up in spring should be used, and they should be treated like mustard — cooked in more than one water. The flavor is good but different enough to require a little practice in order to like it.

Orach is little grown in this country, since it is less distinct than other greens (and there are so many greens), although the white variety is standard in France. Some years ago I grew the 'Red Orach,' which makes a splendid ornamental annual 4 or 5 feet in height. The entire plant is a solid purple-red, and a clump in a perennial border (it is an annual) will certainly add color interest. The 'Red Orach' is much redder than the leaves of the purple plum. The 'Blonde' is more often used in cooking.

One mark of the true gourmet, however, is that he keeps on searching for the best. This requires experimentation, and some of the little-known vegetables may, in time, find a place on his regular table. Or, at the very least, curiosity will be satisfied.

POT GREENS

Cooked greens remind many people of the Great Depression. A farmer who lived across the road from me confessed when better times came that his family had subsisted for a year or so on a basic diet of mustard greens with salt pork and home-baked bread. There were, of course, days when a chicken or goose improved the menu from a gourmet's standpoint. But all in all, the greens and their vitamins were probably a saving thing.

Only two cooked greens seem to have found a steady place in the American diet: spinach and what we call chard. There are winter and summer varieties of spinach, but the flavor is much the same. New Zealand spinach, which is no relation, is worth a try only because it is different. The leaves are small, thick, and filled with water. Chard is very easy to grow and should be considered a biennial, as the flavor deteriorates during or after the second year. Any standard variety will do, but there is one that deserves special mention. It is called 'Rainbow' (Thompson & Morgan). Everyone is familiar with the red-stemmed variety, but individual plants in this seed mix may contain stems and veins in butter-yellow, bright orange, purplish reds, or simple reds and white. The flavor is equal to that of standard chard, which isn't always true of the red-ribbed variety sold here. And what's more, the colors hold even after being cooked, so a most attractive dish can be made from them.

There are improved mustard greens such as 'Tender Green' (Park), which is milder. Turnip greens are often cooked in some parts of the country but have a backwoods reputation. One oriental variety, 'Shogoin,' is grown solely for its leafage. Several U.S. seed companies carry it. All beet greens are edible even though they are not very popular. One is superb for eating: 'Longue Vertes' (Nichols). The root, when small, is used for pickling, but the plant also sends up very large, red-veined leaves that are unsurpassed as a pot herb.

Recipes

Lettuce and Sorrel Soup

1 head lettuce (any of the butterhead type)
12 leaves sorrel
1 large handful watercress (or half handful upland cress or peppergrass)
1½ qts. light chicken broth (about half the density of a jellied chicken stock)
1 sprig rosemary, chopped fine
1 egg yolk
½ cup coffee cream
3 tbs. butter
Salt and pepper

After discarding coarse outer leaves, cut lettuce into small bits. Remove stems from sorrel leaves and discard; chop the leaf blades into fine pieces. Strip cress leaves from stems and mince. Add finely chopped rosemary to these and wilt all in butter for 5 minutes, mixing all the while. Combine this mixture with the chicken broth in a saucepan and simmer together for ½ hour or less. At serving time, combine egg yolk and cream, mix with soup, and serve with thin slices of French bread lightly toasted.

Braised Chicory

1 or 2 heads mild chicory. ('Sugar Loaf' is perfect, since it forms a compact head and is not too bitter; a head of escarole will also do)
1 qt. stock (chicken or beef)
3 small mild onions (silver skins are ideal, but green spring onions will also do)
2 tbs. butter

Parboil the whole chicory for 10 minutes. Taste a leaf midway for bitterness; if there is too much bite, pour off some of the water and add fresh boiling water. Pour through a colander, and thoroughly drain heads of all water. Chop the heads rather coarsely and place with the butter and stock in a casserole dish that can be covered. Add chopped onions and salt to taste. Cover and braise in hot oven for 1½ hours. When mild, the dish is perfect at that point. More bitter flavors are modulated by adding a cream sauce or roux just before serving.

Sorrel Omelet

2 or 3 sorrel leaves (6-inch stage but young and tender)
1 truffle, or three tiny button mushrooms, minced
4 eggs
1 tbs. butter

First remove sorrel stems and roll the leaf blades in tiny bundles. Cut these crosswise to produce thin, short ribbons. Peel and thinly slice shallots (larger ones may have to be quartered first). Dice the truffle or mushrooms into very small bits. Beat the eggs into as much of a froth as you can get from a fork. Heat omelet skillet and butter until the butter begins to brown. Quickly whip greens and other ingredients together, and put the whole mixture into the skillet. (Don't dump it in; you want an even dispersal of all contents when the omelet is finished.) From here on the technique is like that for any omelet.

Chard as a Potherb

Cooked greens such as mustard and spinach can be treated the same way.

5 large leaves each, 12 to 18 inches long, of yellow-ribbed chard, silver-ribbed chard, red-ribbed chard, and purplish-cerise-ribbed chard (ordinary chard will do as well but will be much less beautiful when served)
4 to 6 tbs. olive oil
2 cloves garlic
Salt

Trim the coarse end of the stalks and wash leaves. Don't shake excess water off, as it will be about the right amount for cooking them. Cut leaves into thirds and place in kettle with half the oil, salting each layer. Add crushed garlic. If you are lucky enough to have the 'Rainbow' variety (seed from Thompson & Morgan), keep the colors in separate layers. Cover pot and wilt the leaves with a low heat for 15 minutes. There should be little if any draining necessary, as the pot liquor, if not too thin, is poured over the greens when arranged on a platter. Spoon the remaining olive oil over the top. This dish is just as good served cold on the following day, in which case you may want to center the platter with the following condiment.

A Green Mayonnaise

½ pt. mayonnaise (preferably home made)
1 tbs. parsley
1 tbs. chervil
1 tbs. watercress or peppergrass
1 tbs. choice basil or tarragon, minced
1 leaf sorrel
Several drops white-wine vinegar

Garlic and herbs join endive on the cutting board. (Lalo Obregon photo)

(Opposite) Chard and garlic are the basis of a cooked vegetable dish that is good hot or chilled. (Lalo Obregon photo)

Mash all the seasonings together in a mortar or bowl and then combine with the mayonnaise, mixing thoroughly. Let stand at least overnight for the flavors to blend (it will also keep). You can vary the mix with other herbs such as coriander leaves, and finely chopped gherkins with a little pickle juice may be used in place of the vinegar.

Basic Salad Dressing for Leafy Green Salads

4 tbs. olive oil
2 tbs. white-wine vinegar
1 clove garlic
½ tsp. fresh thyme leaves
½ tsp. marjoram leaves
1 tsp. basil leaves
Salt and pepper

Use a plain unvarnished wooden salad bowl, and never wash it in soap or detergent — wipe it dry with a paper napkin. Herb-flavored oils will in time impregnate the wood to the point where it glistens naturally. Keep both a large and a small salad bowl in this condition. Spoon oil and vinegar into the bottom of the bowl, add the herb leaves, and macerate all together with a large wooden spoon. Let stand for at least an hour so that the flavors will combine. If tomatoes are going to be combined with the green leafage, more basil should be chopped over them with a little salt. The tomato juice should penetrate through the lettuce and other greens before the whole salad is tossed.

Blue Cheese or Roquefort Dressing

Proceed as for Basic Dressing but add 1 oz. crumbed Blue or Roquefort cheese to the greens. Use one more tablespoon of oil and chopped green onions in quantity to the greens. Chopped tarragon and marjoram go well with this dressing.

French Dressing

Like the unicorn, French dressing is not a real thing, but it does exist as a name. If it has any meaning at all, it is that of a dressing prepared and bottled ahead of time and spooned over the salad when served. It might be like this:

1 cup olive oil
1 cup white- or red-wine vinegar
1 tsp. dry mustard
2 tbs. chili sauce or 4 tbs. tomato sauce
1 tsp. paprika or a dash of tabasco or Worcestershire
1 tsp. sugar

Mix all ingredients in a jar, and place in the refrigerator until ready for serving. Then shake the jar to scatter the ingredients as much as possible, and spread mixture over the green salad with a wooden spoon. Since this is a late-season dressing — one to be used when the greens are not as delicate as before — you can vary it with pinches of curry or other strong spices in place of the chili, since clearly the salad dressing will predominate.

6 The Onion Family

All members of the onion family — alliums — belong to a single genus. Their flavors are most diverse, however. Most are used for accents. Onions, chives, leeks, shallots, and garlic are almost as varied in their patterns of growth as in flavors. Flavor, in turn, has a spectrum that extends from the blandness of shallots, which is so subtle that a guest may not detect what you have used, to the onions that make you cry and must be peeled under water.

Where the genus *Allium* belongs in the plant world is in dispute, but in the latest and best book it has been placed in the Amaryllis family. We call the closest relatives of the alliums 'Blue Lily of the Nile' or *Agapanthus.* (I grew up thinking of all the onion tribe as belonging to the Lily family, but times and tastes do change.)

These flavorful bulbs, whatever their proper lineage and classification, are also subject to another kind of controversy. Many people will refuse to eat an onion, at least as they know it. Even more tremble at the thought of garlic and its breath. On the other hand, no one would think for a moment about whether or not to accept a soup or a salad flavored with a garnish of chives. Onions will, of course, get very strong in time, but that can be avoided by early and frequent harvests and by choosing mild varieties. Because onions were used abundantly for generations to disguise poor or even slightly tainted meat, many doubts about them have arisen. I have eaten burro that was only tolerable because of the mass of onions and red pepper added by the cook.

However, these blatant and loud-crying flavors are only a small part of the story. Alliums are worldwide in distribution, and there is probably no cooking anywhere that does not use them. Both the Indians and the pioneers used the wild native species to make food savory on an all too limited diet. The finer kinds, such as shallots, are the most delicate of all seasonings and are prized in culinary systems that include an unlimited variety of things to use.

ONIONS

What kind of onions to grow will depend on the intended use, the climate, the season, and whether or not you want to keep them through the winter. Some kinds are designed to be munched whole, others to be chopped into spring salads or summer salads. Winter keepers are calculated to flavor a stew when storms are howling outside and nothing is growing; they have no delicacy but are robust and welcome then.

For spring there are the onion sets that are so handy and useful. They can be put in early and pulled soon, since the little bulb has already stored up the energy needed to make a quick growth. Thus they will be far ahead of anything grown from seed.

So far as I know, there are only two kinds of sets, a red and a yellow or white (there must be strains, though). I grow the one from the Burpee Seed Company.

Silver Skins. Silver skins are somewhat like spring onions, but their uses and seasons can be extended. The young ones can be used as green or bunching onions, and if not too large they are also very good for pickling. Since they have no preferred season, a little calculation will produce a good onion to mix with the midsummer pickling vegetables. At any time when they are young the silver skins are perfect in salads, and in old age they are still mild in meat dishes.

'White Lisbon' is my preference, with 'White Portugal' a second choice. The latter makes a spindle-shaped bulb; 'White Lisbon' maintains its bunching onion shape even after months in the ground. Both retain their mildness of flavor even into midwinter. Where the climate is mild, either can be grown year-round and dug for whatever uses fit the season.

The Red and the White. Onions, garlic, and shallots are divided between these color categories. Often the color makes a difference in the price, and always the difference is a source of argument. Some people like only the white varieties. In garlic and shallots, the white ones definitely grow larger, which is an advantage to the cook who has to peel, chop, and mince them. Red onions are not always smaller, although some are, and they almost always cost more in a store because they are more seasonal. The best keepers and hence marketers are yellow or white.

The gourmet usually leans toward the red and the pink. I have been told that if I had ever tasted a good imported 'White Bermuda' there would be no question. Since the contest has never been set up,

'Red Amposta' is one of many onions the gourmet gardener may want to try, though it is not the best. (Joyce R. Wilson photo)

(Opposite) Onion inflorescence. Onions should not be allowed to go to seed, but the bloom is beautiful. (Joyce R. Wilson photo)

I can't be sure, but meanwhile there are two red onions that have everything. The Italian bottle onion, which is sometimes called 'Torpedo,' is almost impossible to beat for late-spring and early-summer use in anything. The large bulbs can be sliced into salads or toasted on bread, and the flavor is most mild. Later the same bulbs can be used in meat dishes.

A rival for the bottle onion — I assume that the bottle someone had in mind was either a gourd or a sheepskin — is an onion known as the 'Sweet Spanish.' Many people prefer it, and it does keep a little better, lasting into midwinter. This red Spanish onion, which also has a white counterpart, is globe-shaped and will grow very large (I often have ones that will weigh 2 pounds). They are most mild.

For harvesting, either wait until these onions "break over" of their own accord, or if the tops begin to turn yellow, flatten them by hand. Sometimes onions send up a seed stalk, and it is a temptation to cut it off. If you do, the hollow stem will fill with water and rot the bulb. The best idea is to pull the onion for immediate use, or if there are many, bend them over to crack but not open the stalk.

When you dig onions, they should be allowed to cure for a few days. If cured in the sun, a little straw can be scattered over the top to prevent the sun from cooking them (if it does, they spoil quickly). The purpose of this curing is to dry the outer layers of skin to protect the inner. After curing, any place with good air circulation will do for storage. I hang mine on strings in the shade of an old apple tree because there is seldom any rain in summer and early fall in California. Elsewhere a barn loft or shed will do.

There are two other full-sized onions that should be mentioned, if only to balance the nationalities. In England 'Ailsa Craig' has long been a favorite. It is rather pear-shaped and a nondescript yellowish color. Its advantage must be related to the English climate or soil, since it is a second-rater in my garden. The Dutch have one called 'Giant of Zittau,' and you can get the seeds for it in this country. Besides being large, it is the longest keeper of them all. If you live in a climate where onions have to be planted in late spring and not harvested until fall, that might be of advantage, but where late-summer and fall seeding or planting is the rule, it is not, as it has nowhere near the delicacy of the other onions.

CHIVES

Chives hardly need any comment because they are so familiar. There are no superior varieties, which is odd, since most members of the genus are so variable. They are the most agreeable of plants; they will grow from seeds or divisions and are not fussy about sun or shade. Inside they will do well in a small pot on a windowsill. Remember to keep a dozen pots waiting outside to be brought in. When these pots are alternated, the chives that have been trimmed will begin to grow again outside.

There is no doubt that chives are absolutely essential to any cook for garnishing soups, for salads, for chopping over fresh tomatoes, and for topping an oven-heated French bread. They are never too strong in flavor, which makes them cousins to the shallots, which also maintain their calm under any condition or age.

The same can't be said for another *Allium* species that is called Chinese chives. These are often very strong, which is probably why they are sometimes also called oriental garlic. They have an attractive bloom something like the ornamental onion. The leaves of the ones I know are flat, but since the divisions have been traded from hand to hand for a long time, it is hard to be sure what kind you have. In this country these leaves, which are topped just like chives, usually end up in soup, but in the Far East they are extensively used in flavoring all types of dishes.

MULTIPLYING ONIONS

Often called potato onions in this country, these resemble the wild onions that the pioneers gathered. They grow like monumental chives, and the abundant tops can be cut and used in the same way, although they will have a wallop very unlike the savor of chives. The bulbous root is also big enough to be usable, and it does have a potent onion flavor, so you can dig and divide a few at any season. The extra ones can be replanted and will soon multiply like rabbits.

Multipliers have a short dormant season when the tops go limp. Logically you should be able to buy the bulbs for planting at that time, but there seems to be no source. Nichols sells clusters of the plants in spring, and these start very well. If you are a botanist, the potato or multiplying onion is close to a shallot, but if you are a cook, don't think of them that way, for they are remote in flavor and use.

LEEKS

If leeks grew faster, they would be cheaper and more people would be aware of their delicate flavor. They are the mildest in this genus, and the flavor is hardly like any kind of onion. Although they are painfully slow to mature, they also last well in the ground without losing quality and endure both heat and cold. I try to have some year-round.

There is really no difference in flavor between varieties of leeks; they vary in cold-hardiness, size, and shape. 'London Flag,' or 'American Flag,' which is probably the same, is as good as any. Probably there are even more hardy varieties; Thompson & Morgan in England have one called 'North Pole,' which sounds like snow wouldn't bother it.

There is a stubby variety called 'Monster of Carentan.' It is of a very altered and stubby shape, but the flavor is not different as far as I can detect. It appeals to the cook who has to clean and wash it. In order to blanch any leek, earth has to be heaped up around the plant, and some always gets into the leaves and filters down.

It should only take four months or so to produce a mature leek. If they are grown through the winter, that time is doubled, as I find in my record book that seeds planted in mid-June produced a harvest in February. Transplanting is also a necessary part of growing leeks — if they aren't set at least 6 inches apart, you will not get the full size needed.

Leeks are so delicate in flavor that they can be used by themselves as a vegetable, either braised in butter with the finer herbs mentioned in the next chapter, or baked in a shallow dish with white sauce. Grated cheese and chopped herbs should be scattered over the top and the whole should be cooked until the sauce browns a little. Leeks are splendid in a delicate stew; remember to add them right before serving so that the diner will get an intact quarter of leek that has been lightly steamed.

The most famous use of leeks is in vichyssoise, which is a cold leek and potato soup. Take six of your best home-grown potatoes and chop them with four or five leeks, using only the white lower

(Opposite) Shallots, onions, and garlic are kept ready at hand in hanging wire baskets. (Lalo Obregon photo)

stem. Simmer together in as much chicken stock as you can spare (2 qts. preferably). Salt and pepper, of course. Simmer for about 45 minutes. When done, run all through a food mill, then add ½ cup of cream. Garnish with chives and parsley. It is good hot as well as chilled.

SHALLOTS

Shallots are the real glory of this genus. These multiplying onions from Syria were known and prized by the ancients, but they are seldom used by American cooks. They are scarce in market and usually cost about $2 per pound, which discourages many buyers. This is a pity, as shallots are simple to grow. I harvested 16 pounds last summer from four short rows. Since they keep well, this is all I can possibly use and provides me with "seed" stock for the next season and many braided strings to give away to friends.

Because shallots are quite hardy, they can be planted in the fall and winter in many climates, or elsewhere in early spring. They seem to be more subject to rot than their friend the potato onion, even though they are the same species. Hence winter plantings should be ridged up for a double row with a drainage trench on either side. Many books say that shallots are not particular about soil, but in my garden they like it loose and with an addition of bonemeal. If the soil compacts, multiplying requires an effort unless they are grown nearly on top of the surface.

There are many varieties, but for ordinary purposes the red and the white are best. The latter is larger and easier to chop. The imported 'Jersey' type is very fine. There is a French variety called 'Echalote-Poire' that is even larger. It is not nearly as popular, and despite several tries, I have never been able to import the bulb.

Because the flavor of shallots is so mild, yet distinct, there is almost no end to its uses in the kitchen. The tops can be cut and used like chives when you need a garnish. The savor of the bulbs can be best tasted if thinly sliced into an omelet, and from there you can proceed to various green omelets. Shallots are perfect when sautéed and added to a dish of green beans that is then topped with fresh roasted pimientos.

Even dry beans, if they are the delicate ones like flageolets, will respond to a few shallots chopped into them just before they are done. Chicken or game birds can be larded before roasting with shallot slices tucked under their skin. There is hardly a white sauce or a wine sauce that can't be improved by a few of these bulbs, and shallots are good in salads, of course. In fact, a cook who has an ample supply will find himself reaching for shallots almost as often as salt.

GARLIC

Garlic brings up the rear of this column because it is the most controversial. If I had to give up all but one of the alliums, it would take a lot of thought, but my hunch is that the lowly garlic would be my final choice. A government pamphlet points out that more garlic is grown and consumed in California than in any other state, so perhaps I have some geographical affinity for it. Certainly it is not a matter of race, since southern Europe hardly figures in my family background.

There is a definite prejudice against this bulb, but it can be easily dispelled by a simple test. Pour a little olive oil into the bottom of a skillet and then slice and simmer a few sections of a garlic clove. The aroma is one that you won't object to in the least, and most guests will come in to ask what you are cooking that smells so good. (Doubters should try that test on themselves too.)

The crisp slices of garlic can be discarded at this

Planting garlic cloves. The bed is filled mostly with compost. (Matt Barr photo)

Cardoon is related to the artichoke, but it is the stems that are eaten, much like cooked celery. (Matt Barr photo)

(Opposite) Braids of garlic hung on the north wall of a garden shed. Garlic is best kept in a cool, dry place; the sun will spoil it.

point, but the flavored mild oil can be the basis for an endless series of further steps. It can be a base for wilting greens and other fresh vegetables into a vegetable soup, or it could be the start for a poultry dressing or a spaghetti sauce. For drab stews it is perfect, and for a marinade to be poured over already cooked artichoke hearts, it is a wonder. And garlic doesn't need to be fried; it can be crushed in a press that lets through only the juice. For salads and that great and variable staple garlic French bread, a little squeeze of garlic is essential.

Garlic is not just garlic. There are innumerable strains, and if you meet someone from the old country, wherever that may have been, his will be worth a try. I recall being given one called *hajima* that I think came from Yugoslavia. Generally, garlic can be divided into the characteristic pink and white classes. Here the pink is called French and the white Italian. Elsewhere these names may be reversed. The pink ones are more delicate in flavor and smaller in size.

The Burpee Seed Company has a very fine strain of pink garlic that measures up to any others I have grown and is perhaps better than most. I prefer the pink, but the white ones are more salable to restaurant cooks, as I found with some sorrow. The cook pointed out that if a customer ordered steak smothered in garlic — a matter of ¼ pound — it would take twice as long to chop the smaller pink variety. The whites could be minced with a cleaver in a few random swipes.

He was right but was thinking of a skillet dish, and who would be cooking a steak that way unless the weather for grilling was impossible? Even so, for home cooking a little more time and the pink French type will give a better result. However, for a long braid a white variety may be better. The one in the picture is 'Artichoke Garlic' (Nichols); its cloves peel off like artichoke leaves. The virtue is that one can remove a clove at a time without disrupting the strand. If you keep one of these decorative garlands in the kitchen, it will look well but won't last long. Like other members of the genus, a cool spot with lots of ventilation is the best for keeping. In a warm spot the cloves go through a sort of slow simmer, eventually turning brown inside. Even if the process has only begun, the flavor will have changed for the worse.

Green garlic is not a variety but a delightful alternative. All it needs is the pulling of a set of bulbs now and then before the crop is mature. The flavor is milder and a little different. It will serve all the same purposes as a mature clove, but it is particularly good on garlic bread or as the macerated base for a salad dressing.

Garlic is very hardy, never rots even when fall-planted, and does not suffer from insects as some onions do. Results will be nearly 100 percent good. Even the clusters from a grocer are suitable for planting: divide several heads and save the largest cloves for planting. "Only propagate from the best" is the nurseryman's first principle, and it is equally true in the home garden.

If you grow cardoon in your garden — the plant looks like artichoke, but the stems rather than the buds are eaten — you can try a famous recipe that features garlic. Take several stems of cardoon for each person and boil them. Make a sauce of ½ cup melted butter, ½ cup olive oil, 3 cans of anchovies, and 12 cloves of garlic; combine butter and oil in the top of a double boiler and crush the anchovies and garlic into the hot mixture. The sauce is not poured over the cardoon; the stalks are used to spoon up the sauce a bite at a time.

7 The Classic Aromatics

Without aromatics there would be very few interesting dishes. They are the herbs and spices that create the almost limitless combination of flavors any cook has available. It is true that you can combine different kinds of meats and their broths to arrive at a different flavor. And an assortment of vegetables added to such a *pot au feu* will also vary the taste. But above all it is the herbs and spices that have the magic. The famous *bouillabaisse* soup is a combination of a dozen different fish and shellfish, but even it requires the further addition of saffron, savory, bayleaf, and fennel.

Aromatics are like catalysts — they are small in bulk but large in effecting major changes. Or perhaps they should be thought of as lawyers who alter situations not of their own making. Unlike lawyers, the aromatics almost always change things for the better; like lawyers, the wrong ones or too much of even the best can lead to ruin.

Seldom are any of these flavorings used alone, unless you include vegetables like celery and onions, which are certainly seasonings. Generally there will be a blend of two or more aromatics, and that is when the variations are born.

We commonly call most aromatics herbs. This term is not very satisfactory botanically, as an herb is technically any plant without a woody stem. But the word also has another meaning that is as old as English herbals: any plant of culinary or medicinal value. Rosemary comes from a woody shrub, true laurel is the leaf of a tree, and juniper's flavor derives from a berry on a stout shrub or small tree. So although there is no doubt that Escoffier was right in combining them all as aromatics, or we could even say seasonings, the English term "herbs" will do. There is quite an agreement on the basic few and there is no question about which ones the gardener can grow.

THYME, ROSEMARY, SWEET MARJORAM, AND SAGE

All common kitchen herbs are easily grown, but the gardener should separate those with ascetic tendencies from those that like to live richly. The ascetic perennials include rosemary, which is native to the stony soil of northern Spain; thyme; sweet marjoram; and sage.

Sweet marjoram is a perennial, but from the gardener's standpoint it is best treated as an annual, because old plants become woody and produce few usable leaves. Common thyme (*Thymus vulgaris*) will also become woody after two or three years. Many "native" plants have this tendency to lose all their lower leaves and grow only at the tips, which won't do for either the garden picture or the kitchen. Fortunately the tips layer themselves as thyme creeps along the ground, so it is a simple matter to replant these rooted ends.

Rosemary, thyme, and sweet marjorams should be grown hard to produce the most aromatic oil. This means no nitrogen and only moderate watering.

A leaf from the true bay, *Laurus nobilis.* (Joyce R. Wilson photo)

(Opposite) The branch in the vase is California bay laurel, which is often sold as a substitute for the true laurel growing in front of the vase. The imitation is inferior for flavoring, although it is a beautiful plant. (Joyce R. Wilson photo)

A little bone meal is sufficient for fertilizing, unless you just want ornamental plants. There are many other thymes and a few other rosemarys — notably the prostrate forms — that are good garden subjects. They can be fertilized for a rank growth, but they are not suitable for the kitchen.

In a large container, rosemary will grow to 3 or 4 feet in height. The virtue of the tub is that you can turn it and keep the dead limbs trimmed. Without turning, the side away from the sun will become a little bare, just like the wildlings one sees on any desert. When planted in the ground and left for several decades, rosemary will make a 12-foot shrub.

Thyme will ramble, or it can be kept in a 12-inch fern pan; there it will soon drape the sides. If the pot is set outside, the tiny aromatic leaves will soon be climbing over rock walls, brick walks, or whatever is there. In the garden thyme may become rampant and may have to be trimmed back. The trimmings that are rooted make excellent gifts for friends, or they can set in odd corners of the garden to cover bare spots.

Sweet marjoram is an almost perfect pot plant. The first year it makes a tidy gray mound of foliage that is as attractive as the leaves are savory. Two or three 6-inch pots will probably supply all the dry leaves necessary. If you like to dry herbs and give them as presents, a row in the garden will supply plenty. Sweet marjoram thrives in a gritty soil and makes the best essential oils where there is plenty of heat. It should be mentioned here that "wild marjoram" is not the same at all, even though it belongs to the same genus.

The sage that is used in cooking, *Salvia officinalis*, seldoms looks good in a pot, since it soon becomes very leggy. The naked stems can be concealed by planting midway toward the rear in a perennial border. Sage grows to about 2 feet, so you can plant it ahead and then put alyssum or other creepers in front of it. Garden sage mixes well with the other perennial salvias, such as the Mexican bush sage (*S. leucantha*), which likes similar hot and dry locations.

Sage has never seemed important in our kitchen, and I suspect it holds a place with the prominent three herbs largely because it is perennial as they are. And, too, it is a basic ingredient for sausages and poultry dressings.

Drying. For the most part fresh herbs are superior to dried, especially the dried kind you buy in a jar or tin. Home-dried herbs are better, and it is convenient at times to just reach up for a pinch of one of the dried aromatics. Thyme, rosemary, sweet marjoram, and sage all maintain their flavor very well when home-dried properly, and the same techniques can be used for the other herbs discussed later in the chapter.

First, don't dry herbs by hanging up clusters in the kitchen. The drying is perfect and the decorative value high, but the result will be two parts dust, one part kitchen oils that have settled on the leaves, and perhaps one part of the original aromatic. Drying should be done as quickiy as possible and in a dust- and gas-free place.

All you need is a few pieces of cheesecloth. Toss the entire stem, or plant if it is an annual, into a sort of hammock made with the cloth. The stems keep leaves from compacting and provide air circulation. If leaves are densely packed, which is more likely to happen with succulent leaves like tarragon or basil, they may ferment rather than dry. The result always reminds me of alfalfa hay that was baled too soon.

In a day or two, if the weather is warm, most of the moisture will have left, and the leaves can then be stripped from the stems to complete the drying process. Speed is essential, since dust is everywhere and adds nothing to the ultimate flavor. When dry, place these leaves in tightly stoppered jars or cracker tins.

Leaves always have the best flavor. It is also possible to use the entire plant, stem and all, and often this is what you will get when buying inexpensive ground herbs. However, in the kitchen you want only the best. A compromise often used in European cooking is to tie together a cluster of various herbs. When the esters of the leaves have been extracted the little bundle is removed from the soup or other liquid dish. Even Escoffier used the method, and if the result is expected to be robust rather than delicate there is probably no great difference.

On the other hand, I have never yet tasted a stem that was half as good as the leaf that grew on it. There are sound physiological reasons for the difference, since leaves and stems have different functions. It is probably worth the extra time it takes to remove only the leaves, if you are preparing something special.

TARRAGON

Tarragon is another perennial that belongs to the first rank of kitchen herbs. It prefers a richer soil and has leaves that are much more succulent than those of the herbs just mentioned. Even so, you can dry them, but it will take a larger screen and more frequent tossings and turnings. Tarragon grows as well in a tub as in the open ground, but you must make sure you have the right plant, which of course applies even if you are buying packaged dried herbs.

False tarragon is an annual that is often called Russian tarragon. It is of no relation to real tarragon and of no use whatsoever. True tarragon never sets seeds, so it has to be propagated by root divisions. Once you have these roots, it will go on and on like Bermuda grass, although fortunately more slowly. A small bed or large tub will probably supply all the tips necessary for salads and fish. The tips will soon leaf out again in new growth.

The coarser bottom leaves and stems are not as good, but they can be used to make tarragon vinegar. Place 8 inches of stem in a quart jar of first-quality wine vinegar; the vinegar will extract the flavor. Several stems will make a more tarragon-oriented vinegar, but the result may have to be diluted as the flavor is rather overpowering. A few shallots chopped into the jar at the same time will improve the matter, or a slice or two of mild garlic will do.

SWEET BASIL AND SUMMER SAVORY

Both these aromatics are annuals and are easily grown. The best basil is a summer annual. There are other basils, but they aren't the real thing for flavoring. There is a bush basil and a purple bush basil that are ornamental, but they don't have the flavor. There is also the sacred basil of India. For kitchen work, only the common and the curly Italian variety are worthwhile.

Summer savory is another valuable annual. It has a perennial version called winter savory, which is an attractive little shrub and will supply somewhat the same savor if grown inside in a pot. However, it is not nearly as good, and because the summer variety dries well and holds its flavor there is no real point in cultivating the other for culinary use.

Both these annuals will stand a richer soil than that preferred by thyme, sweet marjoram, and rosemary. Basil likes its feet in something thoroughly rich, and the lusher and faster it grows the better the flavor. When grown hard or toward fall when the days draw short, the beautiful midsummer pungency loses some of its quality and becomes a little acrid.

Common sweet basil can be found on most seed racks; there is no need to look for special varieties. Fortunately, many ways are available for preserving it at the peak of flavor. It dries well enough but does not hold its richness quite as well as the herbs previously discussed. Basil and tomatoes seem to have been designed for each other, even though one came from the Old World and one from the New. In midsummer, basil chopped over sliced tomatoes will make a perfect salad.

The full summer flavor of basil can also be preserved by canning quantities of it with ripe tomatoes, green peppers, a few perfect onions, and a little garlic. This is one of the few times when even herb stems can be left in. Quarter the tomatoes, skins and all, and cook with the basil and whatever else is at the peak of perfection. Run the mixture through a collander, preferably one that has a blade that crushes all the pulp through a very fine sieve, thus eliminating seeds, etc. When canned, this tomato sauce will hold all the best flavors, and it can be used in soups, aspics, and stews or as the base for a good spaghetti sauce to which you have to add only the meat. You can make it as thick or as thin as you like, depending upon how long it is simmered after the pulp is removed. Or the sauce can be varied by the addition of other classic herbs and spices.

Pestoli. Pestoli is undoubtedly the most famous use for basil leaves, and it is also a certain way to preserve the richest summer flavor through the winter. It cans and freezes well. Pestoli is a combination of chopped basil and garlic carried in a medium of the other Mediterranean staple, olive oil. Finely mince the basil and garlic and add enough oil, a little at a time, to facilitate the marriage of the two.

For sauces to be used fresh, some people use an electric blender to speed the process. If you do, place the oil in the bottom of the blender and add handfuls of basil leaves and peeled garlic cloves a little at a time. Keep adding oil until the blender jar is half full of a green mix that has the consistency of porridge.

In making a pestoli to be used at once, add whipping cream and grated parmesan or similar cheese to the blend to make an extremely rich spaghetti sauce. For preservation that won't do, of course. To freeze the mix, only the basics are used. Pack them in small jars, or even freezer bags, and pour a little more oil over the top so that no leaves are exposed. Thus, you can have August-flavored basil dishes in December or whenever you want them. For freezing, it is definitely better to chop the basil than to run it through a blender.

Fresh Basil. Basil's freshly gathered green leaves can be used to advantage in flavoring salads, stews, soups, ragouts, and cheese dishes, which puts it very high on the list of most useful seasoning herbs. It also means that a gardener will need more basil than other herbs. The plants grow well in a solid row, like lettuce or spinach, and stand more crowding. Don't pull the plant to harvest; just cut off the tops and there will be a second growth, and then a third. If the blossom tips are kept from maturing the leaves will continue for some time. Toward the end of summer, let a few of the seeds mature; these will breed true and are easy to gather and dry.

Basil also grows very well in a tub. With a little extra effort it is possible to have a much longer season of the fresh leaves. For that purpose I use half of a 50-gallon wine barrel and a soil that is half compost and half well-rotted manure, which provides enough food for a dense planting and yet not too rank a growth to reduce the essential oils that have the flavor. Basil seeds should be planted thickly, and the seedlings should be scarcely thinned. A solid green mass of basil tips results; these should be plucked only at the top and allowed to grow again. One great virtue of this method is that wherever you live the season can be advanced a month or more by putting a window sash or a pane of glass over the top of the barrel. The plants will be up and growing long before those in the garden have even sprouted in the cold ground. A tub near the kitchen door is also a handy thing, since you can pinch off the usable tips as you enter. The only secret is to provide a soil rich enough to supply dense growth.

PARSLEY, CHERVIL, CHINESE PARSLEY, AND DILL WEED

These are hardly as definitive in flavor as the previous aromatics. Most often they are used as a garnish or as a decorative motif, or perhaps as a combination of both. However, a soup can be made entirely of parsley and chicken broth, and it is a good one too.

Parsley. There are three basic kinds of parsley. One is flat-leaved and sometimes called common parsley, or in Italian, *prezzemolo.* There is a second flat-leaved kind called Hamburg, or turnip-rooted, which does have edible foliage, but it is inferior in flavor. The roots are the main attraction of Hamburg parsley; they keep well, so you can have a parsley flavor by grating them into a salad at any time of the year. Hamburg parsley is also worth growing just for soups, where a little of the parsley overtone is wanted.

The most familiar parsley has the crisped leaves; they can be double-curled or even triple-curled in some varieties. There are many kinds with variations in the darkness or lightness of the leaf, or the curl. One, called 'Suttons Curly Top,' has a particularly long petiole (stem) that may be advantageous if the cook is embellishing a full-sized salmon or bass. These garnishing touches are usually discarded, so it hardly matters whether the stems are fine or superior.

For drying at home, the flat-leaved varieties are by far the best. Their leaves are also open to the full life-giving energy of the sun, which gives them a little taller growth and more bulk in the dried leaves. For the curly-leaved varieties it is best to keep a few pots going.

All parsleys have two difficulties: their seeds are slow, and they are irregular in germination. Soaking the seeds before planting is about the best you can do. Young plants (Hamburg excepted) will not transplant at all, and even those at home will yearn to bolt after the first year. The solution is to keep seeding small pots and tubs so that there will always be a few at hand. Parsley will grow in open ground, but its roots are favorites of gophers.

Chervil. In France chervil is as important as parsley and is often used in the combination called *fines herbes.* The phrase is something of a puzzler since the herbs chosen are not constant. Any combination of thyme, basil, sweet marjoram, summer savory, tarragon, and chervil or parsley will do. Also, several may be left out, but hardly ever both chervil and parsley. When used by itself, chervil is a perfect salad herb.

You can always buy parsley, but I have never seen chervil in even the best markets, so it should be high on the list of plants grown for the kitchen. Chervil is intended for only one year in the garden. It requires a little shade, such as might be provided by a row of pole beans, or even that on the northern fringe of a tomato bed. Chervil is not particular about soil, and it germinates more readily than parsley.

Aromatic dill in the seed stage. The seeds are pickled. (Matt Barr photo)

(Opposite) Dill at the dill-weed stage at left, and coriander at or just past the Chinese-parsley stage at right.

There are both plain- and frizzled-leaf varieties, as with parsley, but to get aquainted with the delicate and expansive flavor, any kind found on the ordinary seed rack will do. Chervil is undoubtedly the most neglected herb in American food preparation.

Chinese Parsley. I mention Chinese parsley only because I am so often asked what it is. The leaves look rather like common broad-leaved parsley, except that some are notched on the round rather than deeply divided. The flavor is not at all like parsley and not to everyone's liking unless muted a bit. It is used in both Oriental and Mexican cooking; in the latter case it is called *cilantro.* The leaves are the herbage of a plant that will later make coriander seed. There doesn't seem to be any close relationship between the flavor of the seed and that of the leaf, but a gardener can explore that for himself.

Dill Weed. The leaves of dill are in many ways more important than its seed. Only the tender, ferny young leaves can be used for chopping fresh or for drying to produce "dill weed." You can purchase it in jars, but it hardly comes up to the real thing. Dill leaves are always useful in salads, and the most renowned is dilled tomatoes, a dish of utmost simplicity. Peel and slice thoroughly ripe tomatoes and cover with finely chopped dill foliage. Set the platter aside for an hour or two so that the tomato and dill flavors join together. For serving, a mound of homemade mayonnaise in the center looks fine, but it is hardly necessary.

SECOND-RANK AROMATICS

For most gardeners the herbs already mentioned will take care of the aromatic flavorings for 90 percent of the dishes they eat, except for regional cooking. Mexican and East Indian cooks will want more cumin seed — *comino* in one language and *jeera* in the other. If you buy *jeera* in a ground form it is likely to be mixed with other seeds, usually for the better. Cumin is no more difficult to grow than caraway or anise seed — all germinate easily in light soil. Fresh home-grown cumin seeds are not greatly superior to the packaged ones, so they should be placed low on the scale of priorities of space and time.

Fennel can be used as either seed or leaf. The wild variety is a bad garden weed and difficult to eradicate, although it is a beautiful plant, with its chartreuse umbels and feathered leaves. But grow wild fennel only in waste spaces; in the garden use sweet fennel, which is easier to control.

Juniper berries are worth growing even if you don't use them in cooking as often as the French do. The edible kinds come from large shrubs or small trees. Use the species *drupacea*, a native of southern Europe. Some species native to the western United States also have edible berries that were prized by the Indians. The 'Utah Juniper' produces berries with good flesh and flavor. Try juniper berries in a stew or spaghetti sauce, and you will soon learn what it will do for the final combination of tastes.

There is one leafy aromatic that I place in second rank, but I'm sure to find argument on that point. Oregano is a perennial that will grow abundantly in even the worst soil. Botanically it is a poor relative of sweet marjoram, to which it is most inferior. Still, there is always a lot of it, so only the tips need be harvested; these will have a milder flavor. They are used in many Mexican dishes. If chopped finely over garlic bread, the added flavor is without equal. Oregano is as variable as thyme when it comes to varieties, so one should choose on the basis of taste before planting a clump that may follow you around the garden for years. Some have a medicinal overtone that will be good for nothing in the kitchen. Any oregano dries well, and its high pungency is at its best when used to mask an overly gamey flavor in a stew of wild meat. Its strength is a drawback in a delicate dish.

8 Saffron and Curry

Saffron and any of the mixes we call curry powder are as much aromatics as any of the herbs described in the previous chapter, but from the gardener's viewpoint they are rather special. Saffron is not harvested like apples or lettuce, and curry powders are not only exotic, they also require several ingredients and a complex method of preparation.

It is possible to buy both saffron and curry powder. Buying saffron, if you get the real thing, is probably better than growing it, unless you are curious. Store-bought curry powder of the floury type is almost worthless — unless you make the effort to import a number of kinds from India. Sambar powder is nothing like the curry from a tin, including the good ones of English repute. *Kashmiri masala* comes in cake form and has to be grated for use. It is imprinted with the letter B on the solid block.

For these exotic combinations you should trust the natives of India, but what they use will not be too different from what you can grow. *Kashmiri* is heavy on garlic. Generally, what the people of India and farther east have is a different set of combinations, so the gardener here has his chance to become a magician on his own, at least in the kitchen.

SAFFRON

There are two seasonings that might be used under this name. One is false and called safflower, and it does impart a yellow color to a dish of rice. Safflower seeds also contain a valuable oil that is a staple in some eastern countries. It is popular here as an ingredient of some good-quality margarines. The blossoms on safflower are also attractive in a daisylike way. However, safflower (*Carthamus tinctorius*) is merely a substitute for the real thing. It will turn a dish yellow, but pot marigold petals will do the same thing and they have a more valuable flavor. Safflower is an annual; you can endlessly harvest the ray flowers or the whole head.

True saffron yields a minute harvest. Safflower and saffron are separated by a whole evolution of things, if the botanists are correct. True saffron is a bulbous (corm) perennial from Asia Minor, called *Crocus sativus.* It is not very different in appearance from some of the ordinary lilac-colored garden crocus; indeed, some crocuses are descended from this species.

True *Crocus sativus* differs from most others in that it is a fall bloomer (not to be confused with autumn crocus, of the genus *Colchicum*), so it should be planted in early summer or wintered over under straw if you have a permanent bed. The essential part for coloring or flavoring is the bright red stigma in the center of the blossom cup. If the style is included it will be about an inch long. The plants are most attractive, even though they are smaller than some recent crocus, and since they blossom when the leaves may have begun to fall, they are welcome even as blooms.

You usually think of planting bulbs in drifts, which is certainly pleasing to the eye, but if you want to harvest saffron, the plants have to be regimented a bit. The matter of harvest is nothing like wheat or barley in which whole heads are cut off. Each individual stigma must be cut out with nail scissors or plucked with tweezers. Thus, all plants must be within reach. The process is a little tedious, but if there are only a few hundred bulbs it is not herculean.

If a box bed is made about 4 feet wide your arm will stretch to the center. The harvest doesn't bother the petals, so the attractive display continues. Because gophers are quite partial to *crocus*, it is worthwhile to add a hardware-cloth bottom to a small bed. A few hundred stigmas look rather insignificant when spread out on a sheet of paper to dry, but there is the satisfaction of knowing that they are the real thing.

To extract the flavor and color, drop a few stigmas into a glass of bland white wine; the alcohol will extract the essence. The color is potent enough to stain a glass, so don't make the suffusion in your best crystal — unless you want to turn it into a conversation piece. An hour will bring out most of the flavor. For a rice dish, pour the noggin of wine and saffron into the boiling water before adding the rice, to spread the flavor evenly.

One advantage of garden-grown saffron is that the peculiar flavor is not as intense as it is when an imported phial or packet is used. Ground powder is intended to be pure; it is even adulterated by a test chemical used to make sure that the peasant grower hasn't cheated with his own yellow additives.

I suppose the mildness of home-grown saffron is due to including more of the style along with the stigma. But the weakness of saffron as a seasoning is that it can easily be overdone. Just a touch should be translated into just a slight touch, particularly in soups; otherwise it will come out roaring like a lion and dominate everything else in your cooking. The breath of a lion may be all very well in nature, but cooking is on the side of culture. And in culture there should be no dominance of one single thing, whether in cuisine or in politics.

CURRY POWDERS

Curry powders are the perfect example of diversity. I used to import several from England. Bolsts' #1 was a little hot and their #2 was very hot. There is also the Madras Curry Powder by P. Vencatachellum in India. That name puts you in the right frame of mind for a good curry dish, and it has some ingredients I can't grow — or even recognize.

Nevertheless, these finely ground powders are rigid as far as the contents go. Bolsts' #1 and #2 can be mixed to make a curry that is hotter or milder, but it will still be basically the same thing. Whether you prepare a dish with lamb, poultry, or fish, the predominant flavor will be the same. On the other hand, the glory of the home-grown is that this need never happen, even if the major ingredients are identical.

To challenge native skills and ancient traditions is always a little brash; the reason that old formulas have survived is that they were found to be good. But the home gardener is not likely to be selling or exporting his packaged product, so he can take chances and admit to a few failures.

There are a few basic curry ingredients that any gardener can grow. Coriander seed is probably the most important. Its Indian name is *dhania.* A very good powdered *dhania* can be imported or bought in select shops, but that is not the best way to proceed. In addition to coriander seed you will need cumin seed, mustard seed (white), poppy seed, hot or chili peppers, leaves of true bay, and garlic (optional). All of these are easy to grow. Some other ingredients are more difficult to grow. Cardamon seed is an essential ingredient, but since it is a tropical plant, it must be grown in a greenhouse that duplicates its home climate. (It does well in southern Florida and certainly in the islands off our eastern shores, where it is grown commercially.) Whole peppercorns and powdered turmeric are also standard. Turmeric gives a familiar yellow color, and it makes a good dye for yarn, but I have never been able to establish what its particular savory value was, probably because I have never tasted it fresh.

First roast or parch the dry seeds. Do this on a cookie sheet greased with a thin film of olive oil. Indians no doubt use safflower oil, but I am oriented toward the Mediterranean. Place the seeds in a hot oven and watch with utmost care. A rich roasted nutty odor is the sign they are ready. A few moments later you will end up with a burned flavor that could be of use only in Guiness' stout.

Combining seeds with fleshy things always requires a bit of tact. Both ginger and garlic will make a home-prepared curry better. The simplest method is to slice these roots into the oil in which the seeds are roasted. When their tartness has been extracted only the savor will remain to be picked up by the cumin, coriander, and mustard.

Cardamon seeds are not always roasted with the others. I prefer to let the flavors blend before grinding. Any kind of mortar and pestal, wooden or marble, will do for the grinding. Whole cardamon comes in a white husk with several seeds inside. Peppercorns, rather than a ground product, should be used. In a marble mortar these seeds can be ground into quite a fine powder; a wooden mortar will give a coarser mix. (Personally, I don't mind a little crunch.)

To get the heat, dried peppers have to be ground and added to the mix. It is possible to cheat at this point by using ground cayenne, but this cuts down on the possibility of variations. Peppers, including hot peppers, are extremely diverse, and there is no reason not to take advantage of this fact. The hot element in peppers also varies with the age of the fruit. Bland ones like 'Hungarian Wax' or 'Italian Roasting' may have just a little piquancy when young, but they become quite blazing if allowed to mature fully.

A gardener can take advantage of these different possibilities. Remember that the seeds of all peppers are much hotter than the fleshy parts, so for mildness take out all seeds before the skins are ground. The best method is to dry various pepper skins and then taste them gingerly before grinding. Only a few plants will provide a great variety. Cayenne or its Japanese cousin *yatsu fusu* are peppers that grow upright and will provide all the fire anyone needs, although if you want to heap on the coals you can always use tabasco.

These are the kinds to use for a curry that makes beads of perspiration stand out on the eyelids. They are certainly stimulating and somewhat a test of fortitude. I myself prefer blander mixes that suggest all the flavors rather than giving in to this single principle. After all, if it is heat you're after, there are some green chili sauces that will nearly scalp you. Any peppers should be dried; it facilitates grinding, and having them on hand allows you to make small amounts of different mixes all year.

Festoons or ropes of dried chilis are very attractive, but use them for ornaments only. Before the year is out they are likely to be attacked internally by a small beetle that has as much fortitude as the beetle called the "lead cable borer."

Pepper plants in pots.

To dry peppers, cut and clean them, and then dry the flattened skins. This process is no more difficult than drying mushrooms. Like mushrooms, a little heat as well as perfect air circulation is necessary to prevent mold. The result is something like a piece of parchment that can be kept in a dust-proof jar and crumbled into a mortar when a fresh curry is to be ground.

Proportions are never exact, but you do like to know about where to start. For pounding in a mortar you might use, in addition to these pepper skins,

¼ cup roasted coriander seed
1 tsp. roasted cumin seed
2 tsp. roasted mustard seed
2 tsp. roasted poppy seed
1 tsp. whole roasted peppercorns
6 to 8 husks of cardamon seeds — the latter removed and ground, either with or without roasting

A leaf or two of true laurel can be ground in along with a shred or two of cinnamon bark and perhaps a crush of nutmeg. Turmeric is almost always included, but I suspect it is only for its yellow coloring.

Whatever the formula, coriander seed is always up front. Coriander is an easy annual that will self-seed. There is said to be an improved variety developed in Germany, but I have never tried it. Its seeds, or the husks of its seeds, look like Japanese lanterns. Since the two are hard to separate, I grind them husks and all.

True laurel is *Laurus nobilis,* a shrub or small tree in Mediterranean areas. It is somewhat tender but ideal for larger pots and small tubs that can be brought inside to prevent damage from severe cold. The leaf is the same shape as our false laurel, but it can always be distinguished by the ripple around the edge.

True laurel is worth growing since the leaves you buy under the name are likely to be California Bay Laurel (which is also called pepperwood or myrtle.) The two are not related, although there is a slight resemblance in the flavor. California Bay laurel is sold because a single tree, which grows as large as an oak, will provide a ton of leaves. The true laurel will yield only a few leaves from time to time, but the home gardener needs only a few leaves and only from time to time, which makes for a good relationship.

Over the Top. Most currys can be improved by adding a topping of finely chopped nuts. Walnuts, pistachios, and cashews are ideal garden subjects and will do very well for this purpose. All that is necessary is to have remembered to plant them while you were young — nut trees take fifteen years to mature. The nuts are all better if freshly cracked and roasted on the day before a curry is made. A blend of chopped nuts is preferred to a single kind for top dressing.

As opposed to these lordly ones there is the lowly peanut, which has the advantage of being an annual. As a garden subject it has no appeal, but it is most popular and easy to grow. In some localities, wildlings, such as hickory or hazel nuts, will lend their individual qualities when chopped over a curry dish. There is something appealing about adding the products of the woods, whether nuts or mushrooms or greens, to the foods of the cultivated garden plot.

9 Our Oriental Heritage

The town where I was born and raised had a very large Chinese population and many Japanese, as well as Armenians, Basques, and a rainbow of other races. When we ate out, we generally ate in the exotic but inexpensive restaurants run by members of these ethnic groups. The idea of eating out appealed to me — not only were there no plates to wash, but there was also the great mystery about the ingredients and the different flavors. At home we had the plainest cooking, but it at least served as a foil for the more savory restaurant dishes.

Sometimes I could recognize the plant matter, such as the pickled grape leaf that wraps up a grain-and-meat mix the Armenians call *kumun body.* The Far Eastern ingredients were much harder to divine. Water chestnuts and bean sprouts were pretty easy to recognize, but beyond that the lights grew dim. In the Chinese markets of Fresno or San Francisco, much of the produce was downright puzzling; what was it and what did you do with it?

The first step in knowledge is to find out a name. Plants are like people and therefore prefer to be called by their own names. Otherwise they remain strangers and you will never find what their interests are.

Fortunately, many oriental vegetable foods are also ornamental plants. Taro root has never made a ripple in my cooking, but I enjoy its modest bloom in the back pond. Perhaps someday we will find that the root is also indispensable. Most of the oriental vegetables are not so strange. The turnip bred by Mr. Sakata in Japan is perfectly recognizable — it just happens to be better and is now carried by most American seed firms.

Most oriental vegetables are as easy to grow as those familiar to any gardener. Often it is only the name that is strange. *Daikon* is a Japanese radish of great popularity, but it is not very different from 'White Icicle' except that it is a foot or more long. 'China Rose' and other winter radishes can be substituted, assuming you are not a Japanese cook. If you are, the proper variety will have the slight difference that may be essential for a particular dish.

An easily grown oriental vegetable is ginger. It is supposed to have originated in China or India, but will grow anywhere. The edible part, the rhizomes or roots, can be harvested at any time for green ginger. In a cold climate the roots can be dug and potted over. The roots purchased in a store will usually sprout when planted; from then on they can be divided like an iris.

Sometimes ginger is hot. The uses of green ginger are by no means limited to oriental dishes. A little ginger grated into a stew, gingerly, will add zest to even a plain dish of boiled meat. If you carry the process a few steps further, on the analogy of nail soup, by adding a touch of cardamon, etc. and cook it in a combination of wine and tomato juice, the result is a sort of pan-national dish with oriental overtones.

Some of the classic Japanese vegetables. At top, *daikon*, a radish that can grow a foot long. Beneath them, bean sprouts. The very long roots are *gobe*, or edible burdock, and there are pieces of ginger root on either side. At bottom are *nasu*, a small eggplant much like the French *aubergines.* (Joyce R. Wilson photo)

SHUNGIKU

The name is strange, but almost all American seed companies now list shungiku under one name or another — often as chop-suey greens and perhaps as garland. The plant is most easy to grow and is an edible chrysanthemum. Shungiku has a modest but pleasant bloom, and the leaf resembles the herb feverfew, but the leaves are much darker. These leaves should be cut before the flower stalk takes shape or you will get too much of the chrysanthemum flavor.

Shungiku is an annual, and a short row can be seeded biweekly for a continuous supply of the tenderest leaves, which should be pulled up by the roots because the second growth is coarse in flavor. The leaves are used in complicated dishes, but to find out if you like the flavor, make a rich chicken broth, chop the leaves to release the flavor, and pour the broth on top for a delicious and simple soup. It is always good to distinguish seasonings in isolation before embarking on more complex dishes.

BEAN SPROUTS

Sprouts from the mung bean could be the symbol for oriental vegetables. They are a delight to the inside or the winter gardener, since they have no seasons. And what other edible crop will mature in two to four days? Sprouts are useful in all kinds of vegetable and noodle dishes and omelets. The mung bean is a tiny green smidgen with a white eye. The larger soy beans will sprout, as will wheat, mustard seed, and cress, but the mung bean is the most satisfactory.

The full-sized soy is said to have more food value, and wheat sprouts are also likely to appeal to those who feel undernourished. Mustard sprouts have a value of their own in oriental dishes or salads because they add that spicy tang in seasons when little or nothing is growing outside. The beauty of the mung bean as a sprout is that the process is both quick and uniform; if a quarter of a cup is soaked overnight before "planting" you will probably be eating them on the third day.

There are elaborate methods for bulk production, but for the gourmet only a few sprouts will be necessary now and then. For that small amount, anything that will keep the seeds moist during germination will do. An enamel or stainless-steel colander lined with a bit of flannel cloth that is kept damp will do. The sprouts can be stored in the colander, under the sink, but since complete darkness is not essential for sprouting, it is handy to have the sprouts around so you will remember to check the moisture. If the cloth dries out you are lost, and if it stays too soggy many sprouts will rot and you will have to sort them out.

The Swiss have recently come up with an occidental method of growing this oriental vegetable which solves the moisture problem completely, for those who need only a few sprouts. Their device is made of three fitted plastic rounds like Petri dishes, plus a bottom chamber to hold runoff water. Each level has a drain valve so that it holds just the right amount of water. Planting on each level can be rotated so that you always have a few bean sprouts.

The device works perfectly, but the Swiss directions translated into English don't make it clear that if you are sprouting mustard seed at the same time they should be planted on the top level, since they take longer and need much less water. You can remove that level and give the beans their daily spoonful. Once you have fresh sprouts within reach, Western dishes made from them will occur to you.

Bean sprouts combined with peppers or pimientos, fresh marjoram, and parsley, and all lightly sautéed and then combined with precooked rice, will produce a splendid dish that tastes as much Mexican as Chinese.

CHINESE CABBAGES

Several varieties of Chinese cabbage have become popular around the world and are often available in American food markets. The seeds of at least three kinds are packaged by American seed companies and can be found on many nursery racks.

Chinese cabbages are not at all like the cabbages of the west — they don't even belong to the same species of plant. It is better to think of Chinese cabbages as close relatives of the mustard plant. Some produce heads, but they resemble romaine lettuce more than the round dense heads of our cabbage, and during cooking they lack the familiar cabbage smell. Also, the plants that are known as Chinese cabbage are not a single variety, which is why there are extra names like celery cabbage, Chinese heading mustard, or chard.

Among the varieties that you are likely to find in the market and certainly on seed lists are the following four:

'Michili' — looks like romaine lettuce, but has a tender stalk like celery.
'Pe-tsai' — another in the celery/cabbage class that has a light green leaf and a nearly white heart.
'Wong Bok' — this cabbage has a head that is broad from the base, and its leaves resemble a more compact chard.
'Pac-choy' — resembles mustard greens and forms no heart.

These varieties should serve the beginning experimenter, but there is no end to the possibilities, since there must be as many cultivars in the group as there are in American corn. Burpee has developed a quick-growing, loose-leaved type called 'Crispy Choy,' and from Japan there are ones like 'Nagasaki Market' and 'Nozaki Early' (Saier has both).

These Chinese cabbages are valuable for their versatility. Coarse outer leaves can be used to blanket a steamed fish; they will impart their piquancy and can then be discarded, but in the meantime they also serve to conserve the moisture within the cooking fish. The stalks of some kinds can be used like celery and combine well in any mixed-vegetable dish. Tender inner leaves can either be used whole in salad or grated like ordinary slaw. Most of the plants can also be boiled whole like an ordinary cabbage, but that is getting the least for your efforts in the garden.

SOYA BEANS

Soya beans, or soybeans as most of us now call them, are certainly a remarkable product. From their seeds it is possible to make glue, synthetic rubber, varnish, and plastic. Some varieties are also edible. They have a high protein content and can be used as an additive to weaker foods, if you are hungry. For the home gardener with a broad spectrum of vegetables to choose from, dietary or vitamin deficiency is no consideration. Peas and dry beans have quite a bit of protein, and many vegetables have more vitamins than the dry soybean.

There are two soya products that are of vital interest in the kitchen: soy sauce and bean curd. You can make your own soy sauce, but since the Japanese do this superbly well, there is no reason to challenge them. The process is more complicated than making a fine wine and the results more dubious. (You can test this by comparing an American-made sauce with the imported counterpart.)

The home-grown bean will make both soy milk and in turn soy cheese or bean curd. To make the milk, soak soybeans for 24 hours, with the shells removed and the pulp ground. While grinding, add enough water to produce a liquid. Next boil that liquid for an hour and strain it. Soy milk has a vogue among health-food people. It is tolerable, and for all I know it may make the soul grow larger or expand the intellect. But more importantly, soy milk will curdle just like cow's or goat's milk. The result is a product that has been compared to cottage cheese. To me the curd is much nearer to what the Italians call *ricotta*, and it can be used for the same purposes. *Tofu*, as soy cheese is called, doesn't keep long (three days unfrozen), so it may be a good idea to try out the commercial versions before grinding your elbows.

There are so many kinds of soybeans that the gardener has a problem. Among the edible sorts these vary in days to maturity and type of growth. The 'Oriental' black bean (Nichols) grows low, and its seeds have a good earthy taste, somewhat like the 'Mexican' black bean that also has a savor of mushrooms. Foliage and bean shape differ, but who knows how many times food plants have passed back and forth around the world?

The opposite in growth form from the black bean is 'Tamanishiki' (Saier). It makes an attractive plant about 4 feet high and is useful as a background plant in the garden. All soybeans will twist up like mesquite or screw-beans and shoot their seeds all over the landscape when the sutures of the pod rupture. For this reason they must be picked before maturity and the pods must be placed in a burlap bag or twist of cheesecloth. Inside they will have their own Chinese New Year with a great deal of popping and snapping.

ORIENTALS ON THE FAMILIAR SIDE

The Japanese and Chinese share quite a number of vegetables with us. Most are easily grown; the only difference is choosing between their named varieties and ours. Snow peas, or any edible pod variety, are important in oriental cooking. Often these edible pods are combined with water chestnuts or bamboo sprouts, but so far as the peas themselves are concerned, any of the occidental varieties listed in Chapter 4 will do equally well.

The Eastern eggplants have a smaller head. In this country they often sell for a higher price than our standard varieties. The Japanese call the little slim ones *nasu.* They may have some peculiar value that I have missed, but generally occidental types will do as well, and you can get them in the same shape. The French *aubergines* such as 'Violette longue' are almost identical to the Oriental shape. I suspect that these smaller varieties are prized because they will ripen with less heat than the larger ones, and there aren't many places where the season will mature a full-sized eggplant.

The Japanese radish called *daikon* is a staple in their markets. It is long, white, and hot. I prefer a milder French one of the same color and shape called 'Radis Glaçon.' (Any radish will get hotter as it ages, so you can calculate that factor.) Large and long-rooted radishes have a purpose: bulk. It is easy to grate them into the preparation. If it came to that, one could use the little round 'Cherry Belle,' which has a fine medium-tart flavor, but if much of it were called for, grating would be a problem and a knuckle might be nicked.

SOME ODD ORIENTAL PLANTS AND ROOTS

Water chestnuts, taro root, and lotus root are aquatic plants. All are attractive even if you don't use them in the kitchen and will grow in any vat of water or pond. Water chestnuts are fruits rather than roots and have been grown for a long time in Europe as well as in the Orient. The ones in tins are equally good, so growing them is a matter of interest rather than necessity.

Taro Root. Taro is more familiar to many Americans,

since it is the basis for what the Hawaiians call *poi.* Taro is a bog plant, but it will also grow in moist soil on nonboggy ground. The "root" is a corm that sends out many little cormels, just as multiplying onions do. The taro of note is a variety of *Colocasia esculenta* that makes an attractive aquatic plant with a dull-purple bloom. I grow it in pots that are sunk in a large wooden container, since it is not truly aquatic and needs soil to multiply its roots. It will not grow as a floating plant.

The young shoots as well as the roots are edible. The latter are either boiled or steamed and made into a paste. This paste is allowed to ferment for a day or two and then is applied to the outside of fish or other meats. (Fermentation in this sense is related to certain cheese processes, rather than to the production of alcohol.) The result is something like bean curd, but more acid in flavor.

Lotus Root. The Japanese call this one *renkon*, and Chinese markets also sell a pulverized flour made from it. The edible part is the anchor for an aquatic plant of great beauty. Botanists call the genus *Nelumbo;* it contains at least two important species, one from the Orient and one native to North America. Ours is yellow when in bloom, and the eastern variety has a white or pinkish blossom. Most people think of them as water lilies, but they aren't, although they probably are some kind of cousin.

My first struggle with this root began when a friend and I spent a few hours, waist-deep in water, trying to disengage cuttings of the root from an intertwined mass in an old logging pond. You can grow lotus root in a sunken wooden tub, and there the gardener has more leverage. If you only want the beautiful golden flowers, the rhizomes will multiply in the bottom of any pond where the freezing level does not reach into the muck in which they are planted.

The flour can be used in place of cornstarch for thickening oriental dishes, but the home gardener is more likely to use whole chunks of the root, which are cooked with meat, traditionally pork, although it makes no difference. The farinaceous quality of the lotus root thickens the broth and imparts its own flavor. Seeds of the oriental lotus are also used in many dishes there.

Edible Burdock. The burdock is a true root and one for garden soil rather than bog or water gardens. Edible burdock belongs to the daisy family, and is thus a far cry from exotic tubers and rhizomes that grow in water. The Japanese call this root *gobo*, and there are many garden varieties. Nichols sells the seed of a variety called *'Takinogawa.'* Soil requirements are much like those for the full-sized carrots, and *gobo* can be used as a boiled vegetable, like a carrot or turnip, but the flavor will be quite distinct.

Chinese Parsley. Chinese parsley confuses so many people that it needs to be mentioned again. It is a native of southern Europe and is one of the food exchanges that East and West have made. Useful food products travel almost as fast as bad news, which accounts for the vast array of New World kinds in the Old World, imported just as soon as they were discovered by European voyagers. There is a similar circuit around the world from the eastern islands to Japan and mainland China.

A plant that began as coriander in southern Europe traveled against the sun and came back to us as Chinese parsley. In oriental cooking the leafage rather than the seed seems to be most used. That use is equally Mexican (in Mexico the plant is called *cilantro.*) Seed packets may have any of these names on them, but they are all the same plant.

Oriental Alliums. There are some onions that are called Chinese leeks, Chinese chives, or Chinese garlic. The first two are varieties of *Allium tuberosum.* All can be cut as you would cut a few tips from a chive plant, but the savor is stronger and different. These onions are better for flavoring mixed-vegetable dishes than salads.

Any good onion can be used in preparing oriental dishes, but one from Japan deserves special mention. It was developed by the Japanese nurseryman Sakata. It is evergreen or perennial, 'Sakata Evergreen,' and a tub of them is the most photographed thing in our garden. It is not like our multiplying onions at all. This variety divides into two and has full-sized leafage. The edible white part is like a super spring onion and has the advantage of being always available in more seasons. If left undivided the bulbs become spindle-shaped.

Chinese Yard-Long Beans. This plant is related to the asparagus bean. Neither the foliage nor the seed resembles our green beans. It does very well in the climate of the tropical South Sea islands and performs only moderately well in northern climes. Anyone who has bought these in the market may have been disappointed because they were old and much too large, but a few poles of them in the garden is something else. They should be picked when not over a foot long; then they are tender and somewhat different in flavor, and can hold their own with standard green beans.

10 Wine

Winemaking is very much a garden project, since it is so pleasant to grow a few grapes. Even more pleasant is a wine that has been made from clusters plucked from your garden, crushed there, and then fermented and bottled by the host. This wine may not equal the best of imported varieties or the choice domestic kinds, but the personal note means something to the guests, and when well made the glass will be a matter of pride to the one who carves the meat and pours out the vintage.

Homemade wines are not as definitely superior to commercial offerings as home-grown vegetable crops. On the other hand, the amateur still has some advantages. The garden vintner will not water the grape juice as it is crushed, which is often done in commercial operations. (It is a perfectly legal way to standardize the alcohol content of a wine, but it does have an effect on its richness and body.)

Commercial wines are also filtered one or more times to give the clarity and shelf-life that buyers demand. This step has advantages, but it detracts from the robustness that you can get from an unwatered and nonfiltered home-grown wine. Of course, you don't want any kind of sediment in the finished bottle, but there won't be any if the process is done correctly.

The gardening winemaker can also make small batches and control what goes into them. By law, a table wine as renowned as Pinot Noir has to contain only 51 percent of that variety of grape. The best ones have more, of course, but because of the price squeeze many vintners add cheaper grapes to their crush. And worse, some even add grapes never intended for wine, to make a cheaper brand. You might as well add dandelions as 'Thompson Seedless' to a vat of fermenting grapes!

You can also err on the side of purity. In 1955 I made up a barrel with no other grapes than 'Petite Syrrah.' Every few years we taste a bottle and then put it away again for the future. It is sound and perfect, but it has never smoothed or rounded out to the point where it is a treat. Perhaps another ten years will do the trick, but a gardener often deals with annuals and expects to see some immediate return from what he plants. A gourmet gardener wants a wine that will complement the best of what he has grown in the vegetable rows, and that doesn't take more than a year or two at the most.

GROWING VINES

All grapes are thoroughly obliging ramblers that

Grapes add beauty to the garden. Picking the ripe clusters is the winemaker's pleasant first step. (Matt Barr photo)

Rosinda Holmes

will climb a wall, shelter, or arbor, or for that matter climb a tree. We have a native variety that has made it to the top of an immense cottonwood in 3 years. It is not there for wine, to be sure, but it attracts all manner of birds in late summer and fall. Domestic grapes are almost as vigorous as the wild ones — the Romans knew the trick and grew many of their wine grapes in the trees around villas and farms.

Unlike ivy and other climbers, grape vines will injure nothing. Their tendrils have a reasonable grasp that does not strangle, and they have no gluey foot like a Virginia creeper. The old stump of a tree makes a perfect support, and it is a pleasure to see the great purple or golden yellow clusters hide the remains of a once-favored garden subject. This means that grapes can be put anywhere and trimmed or tied as needed. If vines are left to climb, you can get a prodigious number of clusters from even a single vine, and several will give you box after box. (It makes no difference that this isn't the commercial procedure.)

Any kind of a trellis or arbor, whether it is over a porch or built apart from the house, is almost ideal for growing a few wine grapes. Near the vegetable garden it provides a shady retreat on hot days for the gardener and provides a place to welcome friends. These isolated grape arbors do take up space, so in a small garden you may want to make double use of an area. A driveway, for example, can be covered with a light trellis bearing grapes. Arbors of this sort are old-fashioned from the standpoint of house design, but they are an excellent way to utilize waste space and provide shade for the house. So why not be old-fashioned? After all, even growing vegetables is either on the old-fashioned or the most modern side.

BEGINNING A VINEYARD

Any amateur gardener is likely to be sent spinning by his enthusiasms. Doubtless you have met a friend who is trying fourteen kinds of convolvulus, twenty-four varieties of cyclamen, and a vast array of crocus species. In a way this is a good thing, and it is certainly an educational process. If the same man turns to grape growing for winemaking, he may again want to try every variety there is.

The beginner should make a small start, because all the different factors will not come together at once — that is why there are vintage years. Twelve boxes of grapes will produce about a quarter-ton of crushable fruit. This should be a plethora for the beginner, since it might produce 40 gallons of wine.

By law, a home winemaker with a federal permit can make 200 gallons, but smaller experiments are wiser. If the first effort is a failure and turns to vinegar, there is still hope. An acetified wine that is undrinkable is still perfectly good for a marinade, since the acid breaks down the tougher meat fibers. In a stew a second- or third-rate wine also has the value of extracting and holding the flavors of various herbs. Wine may turn to vinegar, or it may go moldy; in the latter case it is only fit for the compost heap.

Testing for Sugar Content. If you want to turn the twelve boxes of grapes into wine and thus have a few tidy bottles on the table, there are some devices that will help. Mind you, wine was made for centuries before these were invented, but they do aid. The only scientific device involved is a saccharimeter (a sugar tester) that will tell you when the grapes are ripe enough. A saccharimeter complete with plastic jar can be purchased from

Testing sugar content with a saccharimeter is no more complicated than taking your temperature. (Matt Barr photo)

Nichols for a few dollars. A firm called the Complete Winemaker sells a slightly more expensive saccharimeter and container.

The container for the tester is of little importance since the juice is discarded after testing. The metal tube of an old tire pump will do well enough. All that takes place is the squeezing and straining of enough juice to fill the tube so that the sugar tester can be floated in the juice. The tester is marked off in numbered degrees that can be read as easily as temperature degrees on a thermometer. In this case, however, it is the density, and hence sugar content, of the grape juice that is measured.

The sugar content of the grape juice is important because the alcohol content in the finished wine will be about half that of sugar degrees. It would be fine to have a wine as light as beer, but it wouldn't keep even if tightly bottled. For stability you need at least 18 to 26° of sugar as measured on the tester; 21 to 23° will produce a balanced wine of 11 to 12 percent alcohol, which is standard for table wines.

GRAPE VARIETIES

Most parts of the country are limited to such varieties of native grapes as 'Concord,' 'Catawba,' and certain improved wine varieties of native species. These latter varieties are cold-hardy, which is not true of the European wine grapes that all belong to the single species *Vitis vinifera.* From this species comes the vast array of varietal types of which a handful have become famous. Most will grow in some regions of California (and the lower Rio Grande Valley), but not everywhere there and certainly not to equal perfection in more than a few localities.

Most fine wine varieties require a long growing season but not too much extended heat, so they are grown in the cooler coastal regions. The most versatile of fine varieties, and the most valuable for the home gardener, is 'Zinfandel.' It will do moderately well in Southern California. In cool table-wine regions it is superb and also matures quickly enough for a two-year-old wine to be palatable.

Of the two famous French wine grapes, 'Cabernet Sauvignon,' which produces the clarets of Bordeaux, is the most desirable here. The perhaps greater 'Pinot Noir' of Burgundy does well in only a few places and is certainly not for the amateur garden winemaker. Both will take at least four years to mature, which is a hard thing for the beginner, since one must take into account the three years it takes to bring vines into bearing.

Wines made from white grapes are very quick to mature, and many of them are drinkable in the first year. The production of common white grapes, such as 'French Colombard,' is so heavy that very few vines will be needed, and although there is nothing great about its flavor, there is a fruity overtone that is pleasant at the table and excellent for combining with fruit compotes. Of the famous whites, 'Chenin Blanc' and 'White Riesling' are probably the easiest to tend. For varietal possibilities you should always consult the local farm adviser. Above all, plant one kind if space is limited, because a scramble of everything will produce only a potable nothing.

CRUSHING

Some kind of container to hold the freshly crushed grape juice is an obvious necessity. My own experience has been with the romantic vats, puncheons, and barrels, but a beginner would do well to start with simple plastic garbage cans. These are easy to keep clean, and there is no problem of

Crushing the grapes. This old-fashioned wheel with its gears and rollers works very well, but a tub and a piece of 4 x 4 lumber will do the job too. (Matt Barr photo)

keeping them liquid-tight, as with wooden staves.

Assuming that you have tested the crop for ripeness by determining its sugar content, crushing is the next step. For the few grapes you would use to make 10 or 15 gallons of wine, hand squeezing is possible — tramping with the feet is no good at all. (Just try it once and you will see why!) Cider mills or any other crusher will do as long as the seeds are not also crushed; that will release too much tannin and produce a bitter wine even from good grapes.

Remember not to fill the container more than two-thirds to three-quarters full of juice. Otherwise the violence of the fermentation at its peak may cause the foam and solid matter to boil over. The resulting mess is even greater than when a kettle of jelly is forgotten on the stove.

STARTERS

Fermentation is a natural process, and if you live in a wine country there will be enough yeasts in the air to settle in and start things going. Elsewhere this may not be the case, and if action is long delayed the wrong yeasts may arrive on the scene. Here, in the wine regions of California, the proper yeasts are as plentiful as motes in a sunbeam, but elsewhere a starter is needed.

The old theory was to spread ordinary baking yeast on a slice of toast and float it yeast-side down. The thought makes me shudder, and I understand that it adds a beerlike flavor to the wine. It is not necessary, since there are several easy sources for the best European wine yeasts. These are planted at the time of crushing and set the juice going in the right direction.

How fast or slow a fermentation may be is one of life's mysteries. It may be violent and reduce the sugars to alcohol in a matter of three or four days, not counting the residual ferments that will always tag along. On the other hand, it may drag along for weeks if the weather is cold. Generally, the juice will lose all its testable sugar in ten days to two weeks.

To some extent you can judge this visually, because fermentation gives off carbon dioxide gas, exactly the same way as seltzer water. When the bubbles stop, fermentation is nearly done. It is much better, however, to use the sugar tester; it will keep you advised as to how things are going and how fast.

MARC

The crushing will have of course included stems, skins, and seeds as well as the juice of the grape. These solids that boil to the top are called "marc" or sometimes just "the cap." They must be removed as soon as the wine is done, and sometimes the solids should be taken off after the first few days. Stems have the well-known stemmy flavor and are not desirable at all, but it is hard for the home vintner to get rid of them other than by hand picking.

Whenever the sugar content of the juice has reached zero on the test scale, the pure juice has to be poured into a barrel. Large glass jars will do, but they are dangerous. The last remaining bubbles may build up enough of a head to crack the jar if it is corked. To avoid this, fermentation bungs are used in either barrels or jars. The gadget is simple and can be handmade, except that a variety of kinds are so cheap that it isn't worth the trouble.

The purpose of the fermentation bung is to let the last gas escape without letting any air back into the new wine. Again, the container should not be full of

A home wine cellar dug into a hillside. The temperature can be kept at 60-70°, which is suitable for all operations including storage of bottled wine. (Matt Barr photo)

juice or it will gurgle itself out and over and onto the floor. All you need for such a bung is a bent tube coming from the barrel. Its outer end rests in a glass of water so that the last gases must bubble through to escape. It is one of the pleasantest sounds when there is only a burble or two a minute. If there are several barrels it is like being among a group of dolphins!

PRESSING

Free-run juice makes the best wine, but the pulp that is taken off also contains a good run of juice. The wine press is an important part of man's history. My own is certainly part of my history and that of several neighbors. A press is an attractive piece of equipment. Like a good bird dog it may not be used often, but it is a fine thing to keep about.

There is really no need to squeeze out the last droplets of new wine. On the other hand, a press will produce wine of a most beautiful color; often coloring matter is in the skins, so more of this is extracted. More of the harsher flavors will come along with that too, and a wine with much press in it will be slower to age.

RACKING

Fairly soon after all has become quiet, the new wine has to be siphoned off into another barrel or jar. If you use a jar don't put the cork in tight. Racking is necessary for two reasons. There will be spent yeasts, seeds, and all manner of solids at the bottom; they are no good for flavor. What you want is the pure ruby or amber juice. The second reason is that all barrels or jars have to be kept completely full of the new wine so that no air can get to it. Oxygen will first flatten the taste and then produce organisms that spoil the wine altogether. Hence "make-up," which means checking to see that everything is brimful, should be watched closely. At first this will be every day or two, but later it will stretch out to as long as a month.

During the winter, wine will go through a number of changes. It will precipitate all kinds of things during the process of maturing. The most familiar matter that settles out is ordinary cream-of-tartar. It is valuable in baking but not in wine. Other matters are sediments. Some are hard, and others are feathery. They are the sediments that will send up a cloud as you pour out a glass of wine, if you haven't removed them. They are little dust devils that spoil the whole picture.

A second racking in spring, when the leaves begin to unfold from their buds, should get rid of most of these unwelcome particles. Racking, of course, does not mean pouring from one container to another. Racking requires siphoning. The second racking also requires a good clear, cold day with perhaps a north wind blowing. The reasons for that oddity were explained by Louis Pasteur.

On such a day all the remaining sediments will be at the bottom. To siphon, fix a small rubber tube to a stick just above the sediment level. You can usually determine the level by first gently lowering the stick into the barrel. Solid matter will cling to the bottom inch or two; above that line everything will be clear. Place a rubber band around the hose and stick to hold the hose just above that point.

BOTTLING

By now you have wine. The only problem is how to keep and serve it. For the better reds, two years in the barrel is likely to be a good thing, if there is space. White wines can be bottled at nine months, because they will then have a lingering bit of summer perfume that is lost later. Any bottle will do, but its shape, color, and even thickness have something to do with the final effect on the table. There is no need to buy bottles, since many restaurants will be glad to get rid of them.

European wine bottles will have a great diversity. There are round-shouldered amber bottles from Burgundy, austere greenish-black ones from Bordeaux, sky-blue Imperials from Switzerland, the long-necked *flasche* from the Rhineland, and others of indescribable shapes and tints from Italy, Spain, and Portugal. A handsome bottle will not make your wine great, but it will certainly predispose your guests to look for the best that there is in it.

11 Weathering the Winter: Endives and Mushrooms

Whitloof and mushrooms are a rather strange pair, but both will grow in the dark and in winter, if the temperature is right. Both are extremely choice from the cook's standpoint. You can, of course, buy mushrooms in most stores, but it would be a rare market indeed that offered the true whitloof. Since the requirements are similar, there is no reason not to grow both at once. Mushrooms need a temperature of 70° to germinate and 60 to 65° for development, which is also tolerable for sprouting whitloof, although it prefers 50 to 60° for growing.

Anything will do for a room to house them: a vegetable cellar or a separate house. The most beautiful one I have seen was designed and put up by Clifford Conly in his gardens on the shore of Tomales Bay in California. The waters of the bay keep the temperatures inside in the low 60s year-round. The structure is basically half of a fairly large wine vat, with a plant door and a ventilator on top. Air circulation is essential, and that should be kept in mind if a house cellar is used.

Conly's method is to plant in beds, but most gardeners will find that a flat somewhat larger and deeper than the standard nursery flat is easier to handle since the soil has to be changed each round. Whitloof will do very well on a shelf bed since the food is in the root itself. Light material can be used in the bed, although sand is preferred for the blanched sprout.

WHITLOOF

Whitloof is simply the Dutch name for white-leaf. It is also called Belgian or Brussels endive. For those who don't know this plant, I might say that what you get from it is a little candle-flame-shaped head and about 6 inches of leaves that are white and have only a suggestion of the bitterness so apparent in wild chicories. The leaves can be braised, of course, but their tartness will produce a winter salad that has all the light thunder of a spring storm but not its bite.

The growing is a little peculiar when you think of other garden plants. In the first place, you have to grow the root as an independent body. If you have cut off the flower stem of a tulip the first year in order to get a larger one the next, the process will not seem strange. Whitloof can be planted in May anywhere, and it will send up ordinary-looking chicory leaves. Ignore the leaves, since they are inferior to most other chicory greens. By fall the root will have matured and can then be dug and stored.

The root looks like a parsnip, and the best ones

An endive house.

are a little less than an inch in diameter at the crown. Never cut the summer leafage all the way back or there will be a whole diadem of crown sprouts. Leave an inch of leaf stump for new growth. Trim the bottom tip of the root to promote new root growth. These roots can be stored in a cool place and planted as needed in the dark days. Never plant more than a dozen at a time, because only a few will be needed for salads, and the laws of summer are still at work even in the dark — only recent growth that is tender is worth the trouble.

The fresh leafage is called a *chicon.* To have the leaves white they must be grown through a layer of sand or some other friable material. Some gardeners plant the roots upside down, which seems unnecessary, or they can be planted on their sides. In open ground leave them straight up and keep a ridge of sandy soil over them. Those roots that have been dug and are being saved for further planting should be kept in slightly moist sand and at a temperature below 50°, which is the sprouting threshhold.

If you grow the roots in a bed, a steplike arrangement may be useful. Lay down the first dozen or so roots on the bottom level, then in a week drop back a foot and repeat the process. Since it takes two to four weeks for the *chicons* to mature, three such levels will give a constant and rotating supply during the winter. When the first round is cut off, a second, though lesser, *chicon* will be formed.

Probably the simplest way for a beginner to test his luck is to use one or two lug boxes. If you keep a greenhouse at about 60° the boxes can be set under a bench. Cover the bottom with peatmoss, lay a few roots on their sides, cover with 6 inches of sand, and cover the box for darkness. The best heads are from 6 to 8 inches long, so when the tips have come through about an inch you will know they are ready.

Growing the roots is no problem at all. Plant the seed not later than May so that they will be of proper size to dig before the ground is frozen. Space the seeds or thin the row at an early stage, because the larger roots are very tenacious about their home soil. There are several varieties, but the one sold here on seed racks as Brussels chicory (with "whitloof" sometimes in brackets) is basic. It is also called Belgian endive. There are improved forms, such as Vilmorin #5, but the man at home doesn't really need to worry about the fine points of earliness and marketability.

For those who like to experiment, other kinds of chicory will perform in the same way. The English chicory called 'Sugar Loaf' does very well when forced and blanched, but the head is much looser and larger all around. Roots of the edible dandelion can also be forced in the dark under sand. Use the larger cabbage-leaved varieties or there won't be much reward for the effort.

MUSHROOMS

When someone speaks of growing mushrooms, he always means the common field mushroom or *champignon.* In a laboratory it is possible to raise several good ones of other species, but not in quantity, so those will have to be gathered wild. The Japanese possibly grow the very musky, black one favored in many of their dishes, but most are gathered from under pine trees. The large and splendid *Boletus edulis*, which grows all around the northern hemisphere, including the United States, is also gathered from the wild. Since they are imported — come from Italy — they are often called Italian mushrooms.

Spawn for the *champignon* is sold by almost every dealer in seeds, and there is no trick at all to sowing it, except for the compost in which they will grow. Commercial growers have sometimes used an artificial compost, but for home use there is nothing better than a well-rotted pile of horse manure and straw.

As a warning, it should be mentioned that even horse manure is not what it used to be; it used to be rich, in manure that is. Today much manure comes from race tracks, where everything is kept tidy and the horses briefly pass over the straw on their morning exercises. I can't think of a rule of thumb that will solve this problem, but if a load has a visible preponderance of straw or sawdust over manure it will need to be strengthened before composting. Cottonseed meal, blood meal, or any other high-nitrogen material will assist in breaking down the straw into compost.

If you don't want to go through all this, or you live in a place where it is impossible, there are alternatives. Many nurseries sell flats or boxes that have already been filled with compost and "seeded" with mushroom spawn. There is much to be said for beginning in a small way. It has a second advantage if the mushrooms are being grown along with the endive. Mushrooms require a slightly higher temperature to make the spawn "run" on top of the beds. Seventy degrees or so will do it. Once the white threads have covered the surface a little more compost is added over the top and the temperature is reduced.

As soon as mushrooms appear, a temperature of 60° degrees is ideal; this is the range that is fine for whitloof as well. Obviously it is a good thing to start the mushrooms independently in shallow boxes or flats, in a warmer place, for the first week and then transfer these containers once the white threads show. Incidentally, there is no use in guessing or cheating on the temperature ranges. It is like making butter. If the temperature is too high or too low you can pound on a churn all day with no results at all.

If things have been done right you will always get too many *champignons*. Fortunately they dry very well, as do the wild ones. It is always wise to consult the real experts when using wild mushrooms, including those that may be gathered from the lawn or barnyard.

For drying, all you need is a sheet of hardware cloth hung in a warm draft of air. Wood stoves are great, and a furnace that sends out only hot air will do too. If you can keep this blast at 130° for a few hours it will kill all insects that may be living within. That is fairly easy if the tray is near the ceiling in a room where the heat is from a wood stove. Insects are not a great problem on home-grown mushrooms, but if the mushrooms have been air-dried at minimal temperatures it is a good idea to soak the dry ones in lightly salted water before using, just in case they harbor insects.

12 Saving Seeds for Next Year

Midwinter is not a gardener's best friend, anywhere. It is true that the seed catalogs begin to arrive in January, and you can check these over for spring ordering. Toward fall you always think of what seeds to save and what root crops, fruits, and vegetables can be saved — how and for how long, because they are over and above what has been canned or frozen. There is a reluctance to let go of what is still growing at that time, so you ponder which seeds that have set to save.

The lifetime of a seed is much more variable than the lasting power of an apple or tomato. Some seeds (not all) are very durable. Indian corn in a jar was dug up and gave a fair germination after being buried since 1350 A.D. But the vegetable gardener should think in terms of three to four years at the most. He should label all seed as to date and discard anything over three years old.

There is a covetousness about holding on to the seeds of something good that you have grown. It won't always work, though. Any carrot variety that is to be bred true will need at least a mile of separation from the next kind. Otherwise they will begin to talk to each other, and who knows what will be said. At the other extreme, garden peas are very secretive and will be pollinized, by themselves, before the blossoms are entirely opened. The handy result is that two different kinds can be grown side by side and produce seeds that will be true to the parent variety.

Beans are fairly good about keeping to type, although there will be some crossing even if they are placed several rows apart. Usually these seeds can be recognized. Any old family favorite should be grown as far from others as is convenient. I mention these larger seeds because shipping, particularly if by air from Europe, is rather expensive. Even so, it is a good idea to get a resupply of the true seed from one of the big firms every three to four years.

Peas and beans are self-pollinated, but all the gourds are cross-pollinated and usually combine in a wild disarray, not only cucumbers with squash, but also different kinds of squash together. These combinations are invariably for the worse. Also, no F_1 hybrid seed can be saved, since it is produced by hand-crossing two known strains, which is why the seed is expensive. If you save seed from a 'Big Boy' tomato or a 'Tokyo Cross' turnip the result will not be the same thing.

Many perennial vegetables are increased by division, which means that the next round will be identical. All you need is an outstanding strain to begin with. This rule applies to shallots, multiplying onions, garlic, sorrel, artichokes, cardoon, and some other vegetables. The common relatives of the onion group are annual and "self-incompatible" as the botanists would say, which means that they have to be crossed to set seed — it can be the same variety but must be another plant.

You don't want an onion plant to go to seed in any case, but if it does, don't save the seed if you have more than one kind (and I hope that readers of this book will have a number of varieties). Leeks are similar, in theory. However, there is little diversity in flavor among the major ones, and the tall bloom stalk and flower is beautiful among a plot of okra with its yellow and purple hibiscuslike blooms. One umbel of a leek plant gone to seed will provide all the seeds needed and then some.

Herbs are particularly good about their seeds, and many of them will self-sow and store for replanting. Dill and coriander are very agreeable self-seeders. Scatter out again seeds that haven't been used in the kitchen during the winter; they, and others that are self-sown, are thinned in spring. I like dill among the ridges of onions where a few plants are always allowed to remain during cultivation; I prefer it more for the leaves than for the ripe seed.

Dill grows year-round in my garden, so all I do is whack a mature umbel and let the seeds fly where they will. Basil seed is another good one to save. A few plants will invariably skip by and run to seed in any case. A few heads can be cut and dried, or the seed capsule can be stripped from the plants when ripe.

Compared with keeping a supply of fruits, nuts, and vegetables, the saving of a few seeds is a rather minor thing — you can always buy more. Nevertheless, a gardener is always looking forward. These minor reminders of the spring to come and the past summer are also like the abacus on which a child learns his numbers: they remind you of mistakes, successes, and changes to be made. During this in-between period a gardener can winter over on the preserves from summer, whether they are in the fruited stage, are seed capsules, or are merely ideas.

Sources of Seeds, Equipment, and Information

Gourmet Seed

This list is for the hard-to-find varieties; many excellent kinds are sold by most seed companies. Since the reader will find these for himself in catalogs and seed racks there is no need to list them here.

Nichols Garden Nursery, 1190 North Pacific Highway, Albany, Oregon 97321.
  Many rare seeds. Shallots and multiplier onions. Herb plants.
Le Jardin du Gourmet, P.O. Box 119, Ramsey, N.J. 07446.
  Specializes in importing "Jersey type" (referring to the island off France and not the state) and also imports flageolet and a few other seeds.
Harry Saier, Dimondale, Mich. 48821.
  Has a good selection of both Oriental and European vegetable seeds.
Brecks of Boston, Boston, Mass.
  Imports several of the Dutch varieties mentioned in this book.
Park Seed Co., Greenwood, S.C. 29646.
  Not a specialist in imports, but does carry Dutch half runner beans, and *Lagenaria longissima* squash.
W. Atlee Burpee Co., Philadelphia Pa. 19132; Clinton, Iowa 52732; Riverside, Calif. 92502.
  Has a very good pink garlic and several of the seeds mentioned.

ENGLAND

Sutton's Seeds Ltd., Reading RGG 1AB Berks., England.
  The list is choice and their shipments are prompt.
Thompson & Morgan, London Road, Ipswich, Suffolk, England.
  Like Sutton's, has a very extensive list. These two English firms often carry different items, so both catalogs will be a needed pleasure.

For the other British seed firms see the list of specialists in Hill's *Good Taste Guide* and Organ's *Rare Vegetables,* listed below under Recommended Books. It might be noted that much of the best Dutch seed is available through English firms.

FRANCE

As in England, there are two major seedsmen. It is worth buying seed just to get the color-illustrated catalogs showing various vegetables. There is no problem with language or payment; they are most courteous and very rapid in mailing export orders.

Vilmorin-Andrieux, 4, Quai de la Mégisserie, Paris, 1er, France.
Georges Delbard, 16, Quai de la Mégisserie, Paris, 1er, France.

Export shipping is from country stations, but a catalog will include a properly addressed envelope and a printed sheet of varieties, so that all you have to do is to make a check mark opposite your choice.

Herb Plants

Herb seeds are available everywhere. Mail-order sources of growing plants:

Hilltop Herb Farm, Box 866, Cleveland, Texas 77327.
Merry Gardens, Camden, Maine 04843.
Nichols Garden Nursery, 1190 North Pacific Highway, Albany, Oregon 97321.
Sunnybrook Farms Nursery, 9448 Mayfield Road, Chesterland, Ohio 44026.

Sprouts

Miracle Exclusives Inc., 16 West 40th Street, New York, N.Y. 10018.
  In addition to Mung beans, this firm sells the seeds of mustard and cress, which can also be sprouted, and a Swiss device called a Bio-snacky that is used to sprout these and other seeds.
Wallace House, P.O. Box 288, Gladstone, Oregon 97207.

Winemaking Supplies

The Compleat Winemaker, P.O. Box 2470, Yountville, Calif. 94599.
  Carries all sorts of equipment, from books to barrels to bottles.
Nichols Garden Nursery, 1190 North Pacific Highway, Albany, Oregon 97321.
  Carries some supplies, notably dried wine yeasts.

World's Shortest French Dictionary

One need not know French to use a French seed catalog, but a few basic words and names may help. *Potager* refers to a kitchen garden, and *fourrage* to fodder, i.e. for livestock, so when beets, carrots, turnips, and so on are listed as *fourragères,* take the hint. *Légume* is used in a general way to mean vegetable, although it may also have our limited sense of a member of the pea family. It might be useful to know that *d'hiver* refers to winter and *d'été* to summer varieties.

Some names, such as *carotte* or *oignon,* are obvious. A few that are less so:

ail — garlic
aubergine — eggplant
betterave — beet
cerfeuil — chervil
choux — cabbage
cornichon — gherkin (as opposed to *concombre,* cucumber)
courge — squash (*courgette* is a little squash of the zucchini type; *giraumon* — our turban; *potiron* — pumpkin)
épinard — spinach
fève — English broad bean
haricots — beans in general *(haricots verts* — green beans; *haricots nains* — dwarf beans; *haricots à rames* — runner or pole beans; *grains* — seeds; *sec* — dry; *mangetout* — edible pod)
laitue — lettuce
mâche — corn salad, or lamb's lettuce
navet — turnip
oseille — sorrel
pissenlit — dandelion
poireau — leek
poivron — pepper

That should get one started well enough. If you happen to want to know the name for Jerusalem artichoke, it is *topinambour*. Take it from there.

Recommended Books

Shewell-Cooper, W. E. *The Complete Vegetable Grower.* London: Faber & Faber, 1967 (paperback).
Contains nearly 300 pages of general information and lists of varieties popular in England.

Vercier, Joseph. *Culture Potagère.* Paris: Librairie Hachette.
First published early in this century but still in print some 300,000 copies later. Lists of varieties are good, but need some supplementing from modern catalogs.

Lachaud, M. *Le Jardin Potager de L'Amateur.* Paris: Editions Borneman.
A rather slight little booklet, but it lists varieties used by the modern home gardener in France.

Organ, John. *Rare Vegetables for Garden and Table.* London: Faber & Faber, 1960.
Many of the vegetables discussed are rare in England but common here — okra, for instance. Others are rare anywhere. Overall it contains a lot of useful information. Harry Saier (Dimondale, Mich. 48821) sells it in this country.

Hills, Lawrence D. *Good Taste Guide to Garden Fruit and Vegetable Varieties,* 1969. Henry Doubleday Research Assn. 20, Convent Lane, Bocking, Baintree, Essex, England.
These pamphlets give the results of a gardener's opinion poll, much like our All America Selections. Well worth looking into.

Masefield, G. B., et al. *The Oxford Book of Food Plants.* New York: Oxford, 1969.

Vilmorin-Andrieux. *The Vegetable Garden.* London, 1885, etc.
This massive tome, translated into English from the French, is a classic but hard to find.

Burr, Fearing, Jr. *Garden Vegetables and How to Cultivate Them.* Boston: Tilton, 1866.
Another old-timer, but useful for finding out what was grown here a century ago. Some things new are also old.

Carleton, R. Milton. *Vegetables for Today's Gardens.* New York: Van Nostrand Reinhold, 1967

Sunset Vegetable Garden Book. San Francisco: Lane Pub. Co., 1950
A handy compendium of general information, particularly for those in the western states.

There are any number of government pamphlets of use to the vegetable gardener. These can be obtained from the Superintendent of Documents, Washington, D.C. 20402. They are listed in a catalog called:
Plants. Price list 44, 60th edition, 1970.
One item that a beginner would find handy is:
Suburban and Farm Vegetable Gardens (Home and Garden Bulletin #9. U.S. Dept. of Agriculture).

Index

Note: Italicized page references indicate illustrations.